man's
two natures,
human and divine

Cover illustration: a crystal

ISBN 2-85566-253-2

Omraam Mikhaël Aïvanhov

man's two natures, human and divine

Translated from the French

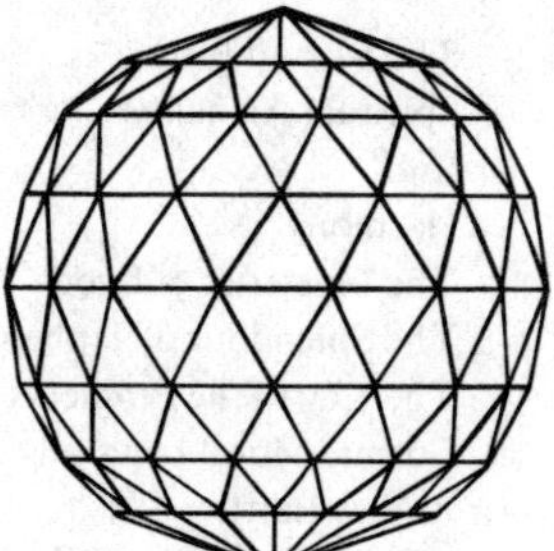

Collection Izvor
No. 213

EDITIONS PROSVETA

By the same author:
(translated from the French)

Izvor Collection

201 - Toward a Solar Civilisation
202 - Man, Master of his Destiny
203 - Education Begins Before Birth
204 - The Yoga of Nutrition
205 - Sexual Force or the Winged Dragon
206 - The Universal White Brotherhood is not a Sect
207 - What is a Spiritual Master?
208 - Under the Dove, the Reign of Peace
209 - Christmas and Easter in the Initiatic Tradition
210 - The Tree of the Knowledge of Good and Evil
211 - Freedom, the Spirit Triumphant *(forthcoming)*
212 - Light is a Living Spirit
213 - Man's Two Natures, Human and Divine
214 - Hope for the World: Spiritual Galvanoplasty

"Complete Works" Collection

Volume I	-	The Second Birth
Volume II	-	Spiritual Alchemy
Volume V	-	Life
Volume VI	-	Harmony
Volume VII	-	The Mysteries of Iesod
Volume X	-	The Splendour of Tipheret
Volume XI	-	The Key to the Problems of Existence
Volume XII	-	Cosmic Moral Laws
Volume XIII	-	A New Earth Prayers, methods, exercises, formulas
Volume XIV	-	Love and Sexuality (part I)
Volume XV	-	Love and Sexuality (part II)
Volume XVII	-	"Know Thyself" (part I)
Volume XXV	-	Aquarius, Herald of the Golden Age (part I)
Volume XXVI	-	Aquarius, Herald of the Golden Age (part II)
Volume XXIX	-	On the Art of Teaching From the Initiatic Point of View (part III)

TABLE OF CONTENTS

EDITOR'S NOTE

The reader is asked to bear in mind that the Editors have retained the spoken style of the Maître Omraam Mikhaël Aïvanhov in his presentation of the Teaching of the great Universal White Brotherhood, the essence of the Teaching being the spoken Word.

They also wish to clarify the point that the word *white* in Universal White Brotherhood, does not refer to colour or race, but to purity of soul. The Teaching shows how all men without exception (universal), can live a new form of life on earth (brotherhood), in harmony (white), and with respect for each other's race, creed and country... that is, Universal White Brotherhood.

1

HUMAN NATURE OR ANIMAL NATURE?

Every being comes into the world bearing within him the tendencies and appetites he has inherited from the dark past, when animal instincts controlled him and installed their power over him once and for all. We can never be absolutely free of the past, the difference between people being that some are enlightened and learn how to control and subjugate their brute instincts with the help of Initiatic Science, whilst others refuse the light or are deprived of it for some reason and remain as they are, restricted to their lower nature. These people think the Initiatic Science unnatural, abnormal, but the higher Beings believe it to be the only natural science.

The majority of human beings belong to the group without light. They talk about rediscovering Nature and obeying the natural laws, but *which* nature are they talking about? There are two natures in man, one lower, one higher. People think they are obeying Nature when in fact they are doing something exactly opposite to their higher Nature, whereas others concentrate on their divine Nature and do everything in their power to subjugate and restrict the impulses of their human nature. Confusion reigns in people's minds and that is why it is so important to make them realize that a higher Nature exists in them, which expresses itself quite differently from the human nature they inherited from the animal kingdom. You hear people say (to justify their weaknesses), "It's human nature!" What they should say is "animal nature", and nowhere is it written that man is justified in giving in to his primitive instincts.

The thing that interests animals most is survival, they need food and shelter above all, and then they need to reproduce and defend themselves. Nature herself has given them their instincts of self-preservation, aggressivity, reproduction, for a reason: it is *natural* for animals to be egotistical, cruel, fearful, but humans are a different matter. Cosmic Intelligence gave them the power to think and to reason (along with other qualities and virtues) in order for them to go further than their instincts alone would permit. They have their animal nature, but they have another nature as well; it is their destiny to develop that nature and allow it to express itself. I am not saying it is easy, nor that it can be done in a day. Human nature is too close to animal nature for it to change easily or rapidly.

Observe yourself and you will see that some tendencies are so deeply rooted that nothing will remove them and at the same time other tendencies need constant encouragement and even, without prayer and meditation, disappear entirely. When you are faced with hunger or thirst, the need for sleep or certain pleasures, no one needs to remind you, you know what to do, those needs are so firmly rooted that even if you wanted to you could not shake them. But when it is a question of reasoning, of thinking something through, of being wise and foresighted, of showing a little generosity or unselfishness, there you need to be encouraged. We have something in us that is very firmly rooted, something solid and unalterable that can get along perfectly well without help... and we have something else in us which is delicate and tender and needs protection. Yes, for centuries man's instinctive nature has had time to grow and become a strong habit, whereas his mind and the ability to reason are comparatively recent acquisitions. Actually wisdom appeared before all other manifestations but as it came from very far away, it took a long time to manifest itself. Wisdom existed before the Creation.

In the Bible it says, "I Wisdom... the Lord

possessed me in the beginning of His way, before His works of old. I was set up from everlasting, from the beginning, or ever the earth was. When there were no depths I was brought forth; when there were no fountains abounding with water; before the mountains were settled, before the hills was I brought forth, while as yet He had not made the earth, nor the fields, nor the highest part of the dust of the world. When He prepared the Heaven, I was there; when He set a compass upon the face of the depth; when He established the clouds above; when He strengthened the fountains of the deep; when He gave to the sea His decree that the waters should not pass His commandment; when He appointed the foundations of the earth, then I was by Him, as one brought up with Him, and I was daily His delight, rejoicing always before Him...."

Wisdom was the first to appear, but not until recently did it install itself in man, that is why it is so fragile and delicate, whereas instinct has been firmly ensconced since the dark ages. It should not surprise you therefore, to learn that you are controlled by your human nature! It is your own instinct, your own prehistoric nature answering to whatever attracts it, without thinking. In order to justify yourself, you say, "Something pushed me, it was not my fault, some outside influence made me make those foolish mistakes";no, all influence is the result of something in you which attracts it, all men carry their animal past within, in the shape of cruelty for some, sensuality and greed for others. The question is how to develop our intelligence and make it strong enough to conquer our ancient instincts and impulses, our animal (or human) nature. It is your problem and my problem and everyone else's problem. We must all resolve it by learning how *not* to capitulate to the lower nature.

Of course the lower nature is extremely powerful but, simply because it is strong enough and firmly enough anchored to have the upper hand is no reason to capitulate. Its strength comes from having had so much time to become deeply engrained, the reason it is so cruel, wicked and selfish is because it has had eons of time in which to become that way, and because it has lived under very difficult conditions. Take animals and what they have to confront in order to survive, all the trouble they have in finding food, a safe shelter, protection from other animals. How do you expect this nature which has lived in such very difficult conditions, to be gentle, good, merciful? No, it *had* to be selfish, cruel and vindictive in order to survive, with the result that now it manifests those things perfectly!

The lower nature has had a right to its place in the sun, it has worked hard and well but it is not the last stage, the peak of human development! It is now the turn of reason and intelligence to manifest. Take fear as an example: fear is very strong in animals, Nature has given animals the instinct of fear to make them conscious of danger, to force them to protect themselves. Nature is a good guide, she saves creatures by teaching them, all creatures must start out fearful. Later, when they are more advanced in their evolution, Cosmic Intelligence intervenes and promotes them by replacing fear with intelligence: it is better to know, to learn, to understand, than to be afraid and remain ignorant. Animals, not being intelligent, must be fearful in order to avoid danger; man, who has intelligence (the new element proving his progress), should not hold on to fear, it is no longer natural because it keeps him from evolving.

It is a law that Nature approves of certain things at certain times and then rejects them, she no longer approves them; we also do that, we work with all our strength to obtain certain things and then we work equally hard to get rid of them! Wisdom lies in knowing how long to keep things and when to let them go. Now do you see why man must give up fear?

Another example: a boy who is attracted to a girl wants to pounce upon her... which is "natural". Yes, but if he keeps on doing that kind of thing, obeying that nature, he will never rise above the animal stage. It is time the other Nature stepped in and advised, "Control yourself! Learn to dominate your animal nature, it will be to your advantage to do so." The higher Nature is, I suppose, an unnatural nature! Someone needs something his neighbour has: his human nature pushes him into going to take it, he *needs* it and he takes it, without fuss, without scruple. But if the higher Nature steps in at that point, and says, "No, no, it belongs to someone else, you must not take it from him, you have no right... and if you do take it, you will have to pay!", then that is intelligence speaking, that is morality.

Men follow their nature, but the question is, which nature, their animal (human) nature or their divine Nature? Unfortunately for them, most people are firmly attached to their animal nature, yes, sincerely and honestly loyal to it, convinced it is the nature to follow, and the day someone tries to make them understand that they have another nature which they should be following, life becomes complicated indeed! But it must be so: the building our ancestors took so many centuries to build was magnificent for that era, but now the time has come when it is worn out and must be torn down and another one built in its place. A building can be right under certain conditions but when those conditions change, it is no longer suitable. Certain elements are preserved and used for the new construction, in the way that builders save beams, iron works, carved wood, etc... from old buildings they tear down.

Jesus said, "Unless ye die ye shall not live." Yes, we must die in order to live, die as far as the lower nature is concerned, to be born again in the higher Nature, just as the seed must die in the earth in order to begin to grow. If it does not die, that is, if it remains stagnant and useless in the attic (which is another kind of death) it will not live, that is, it will never bear fruit. We too, if we remain stagnant and refuse to grow out of our old customs and concepts, we too will never really live. We must die to the old form and adopt the new, more beautiful form, then we will be alive! Do not think Christ wanted us to die, no, "Unless ye die," means, unless we change the forms, the customs, our way of thinking. He who said, "I am the Resurrection and the life", would not have asked us to die, rather He wanted us to become alive in the way He is alive! We have only one way open to us: to die in our lower nature and be born again in our divine Nature.

2

THE LOWER SELF IS A REFLECTION

For centuries, for millenniums, men have been studying the psychic world, trying to discover more about their inner self and what motivates its actions. To aid them, they divided man into different sections. Some divided him in half, using the number 2 as the equation to designate spirit and matter, masculine and feminine, positive and negative, heaven and earth, good and evil, and so on. Others chose to divide man in three: the mind, the emotions and the will, in similar fashion to the Christian spirit, soul and body. Alchemists preferred to divide him in four, symbolizing the 4 elements: earth, water, air, and fire. Astrologers divided him in 12, representing the 12 constellations. Hindus and Theosophists chose to divide him in 7, the 7 bodies: physical, etheric, astral, mental, Causal, Buddhic, Atmic. Kabbalists divided him in 3, or 4, or 9, or 10. To others, man is an indivisible unity. All are true, depending on the angle from which you look at him.

To make it simpler, let us say that a human being is a perfect unity but that the unity is polarized, that is, there are two manifestations, two different aspects. Man has two different natures, the lower nature and the higher Nature, both endowed with faculties enabling him to think, feel and act, but in opposite directions. I have called these two natures the *personality* and the *individuality*.

What we must understand first of all is that even if the lower nature is indeed different from the higher Nature, it nevertheless has its origins above, in the Spirit. Spirit is the beginning, the origin of everything... a fact you must always bear in mind. But when the Spirit wishes to manifest it has to avail itself of a heavier vehicle adapted to the dense regions of matter into which it wishes to descend. These vehicles are called bodies. From the subtlest and most delicate to the thickest and most obtuse, they are: the Atmic, Buddhic and Causal bodies of our higher Nature, or individuality, and the mental, astral and physical bodies which form our lower nature, or personality. The physical (material) body, the astral (emotional) body, and the mental (intellectual) body, are the same thing on a lower plane as the three higher bodies.

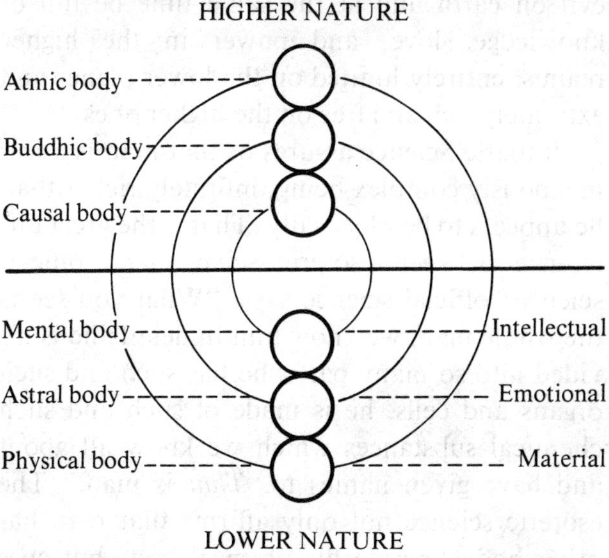

You say, "But why is it that the personality, if it is a reflection of the individuality, is so weak and limited, so subject to error?" The answer is that the individuality is made of the same essence as Spirit: it lives in the heavenly regions in complete freedom, in brilliant light, in perfect happiness and peace, and has every power save one: the ability to express itself in the lower regions of matter, *unless* the three lower bodies (the personality) allow it to. The individuality can express itself in the dense regions of matter only to the extent that the personality is willing. A person may be weak and ignorant, cruel and evil on earth and at the same time be full of knowledge, love, and power in the higher realms, entirely limited on the lower planes and extremely rich and free on the higher ones.

Initiatic Science assures us that man is a tremendously complex being, infinitely richer than he appears to be physically. That is the great difference between esoteric science and official science: official science says, "What you see is the whole man, we know him in detail: he is divided into so many parts, he has such and such organs and cells, he is made of such and such chemical substances which we know all about and have given names to. *That* is man." The esoteric science not only affirms that man has other bodies beside his physical body but goes on to explain the nature and function of each body.

For the moment, even if the individuality wanted to manifest itself in the dense and dark regions of the personality, it could not do so to any great extent. It will take more time, more experimenting, more training and studying and experience over the centuries to come, perhaps millenniums, before the bodies that form the personality can express the qualities and virtues of the individuality. But the day the mental body becomes subtle and penetrating enough to understand the divine Wisdom, then the astral body will display its most noble and unselfish sentiments, the physical body will be given every opportunity for action, and nothing will resist it.

Although there is no real separation between the two natures, the individuality is always seeking to influence the personality toward the good, but the personality only wants to be independent and free, it will obey no one but its own impulses, almost never those from above. Despite the fact that the personality is animated and fed by the individuality, it opposes it steadily until the day when finally, due to the efforts of the one who works determinedly and tenaciously in that direction, at last the individuality succeeds in slipping into the personality and assuming control. The personality then becomes obedient and submissive, one with the individuality. That is the true fusion, the true marriage, the true love, the true esoteric meaning of the expression "making the two ends meet." At one end is the personality, triple-headed as Cerberus, the three-headed dog guarding the entrance to Hell... and at the other end is the individuality, our higher Self, the trinity of our divine Nature.

This union, this most desirable marriage must take place one day... but when? For each one it will be different. In the meanwhile, it is the task of the disciple to learn to submit the personality to the individuality during all the trials and tribulations of his life, to acquiesce to the divine Will above him and become a willing, docile instrument in the hands of God. That is the goal, the one aim of all the exercises and methods we learn and practice in an Initiatic School.

We come from God, we begin in God, everything, including our lower nature, begins with God. Suppose for the moment that you are a gold seeker. Once the ore is obtained, the metal must be extracted before you can see the gold. They appear to be different, the gold and the ore and the matrix, but actually they all have the same origin, because all matter has the same origin. "But," you say, "how did God whose Nature, whose substance is quite other than matter, how did God create anything so dense, so dark and heavy?" The answer is simple. For God it was exactly the same as for the spider when it spins its web. Yes, the spider demonstrates the way in which God created the world! You say, "Is a spider *that* intelligent?" I do not know how many degrees a spider has, but if you will observe it closely no doubt you too will be able to draw philosophic conclusions that will be helpful. Look at it spinning its web! It creates its own universe, geometrically, mathematically perfect. How? Well, the spider secretes a liquid which hardens and forms a fine, supple elastic thread: that is what the web is made of. Snails are equally instructive. A snail has a flabby soft body, whereas its shell is quite hard; at first there seems to be no connection between the snail and its shell, and yet it was the snail that secreted the shell. Little by little, by penetrating the microscopic openings in its etheric body, it spreads the particles apart and stretches the shell. The snail remains separate from its shell, but secretes the substance the shell is made of and keeps adding to it to make it bigger.

This illustration should help you to understand the way in which God created the world: He emanated a subtle matter that solidified. You say, "What dull stories." Perhaps, but in time the most learned people in the world will queue up to hear them! In appearance, the snail and its shell are two different things, but actually they are made of the same substance. Would it surprise you to hear that it is the same thing for the individuality and the personality? The personality is thick and heavy, hard as a shell, and the individuality is soft and light, alive, plastic. They are not the same, but they both emanate from the same thing.

The higher Self, the ego or individuality, forms a body, a vehicle for itself (the personality) in exactly the same way as the snail forms its shell. It is our house, our home, we live inside. The only regrettable thing is that man has identified with his shell, his house or vehicle, instead of with the powerful factor that formed him originally, the Spirit, the individuality. This is the reason for his weaknesses and limitations, his impotence, his mistakes. The body is not the man, it is only his car, his horse, an instrument, a dwelling place. The real man is the Spirit, all-powerful, unlimited, omniscient Spirit. When man changes and identifies himself with his Spirit, he will become powerful, illumined, immortal, divine.

For make no mistake, you are all divinities. Yes, divinities. You belong to a high place in which no limitations, no darkness, no suffering or sorrow, no discouragement exist, where you are surrounded by plenitude. Here on earth you are not surrounded by plenitude because you have not been able to live and manifest life on earth as it is above: the personality prevents you! Obtuse as it is, ill-adapted as it is, ill-tuned as a radio that cannot pick up the essential broadcasting stations, the personality still can keep you from receiving the waves and currents from the higher regions. The divine currents sent out by Cosmic Intelligence are so short and rapid and the matter of the personality so dense and heavy that you cannot possibly vibrate intensely enough or rapidly enough to hear them, they slip by without leaving a trace of what you actually experience in the higher regions of your being. There is a way to improve the situation: by deciding to obey Nature and lead a pure life. If you want more than anything to become a child of God, then your heart will become more generous, your mind more enlightened, your will stronger and more determined; your personality will be only the instrument that expresses the sublime life of the individuality... to the extent of becoming united with it... and then there will be no more personality, the personality and the individuality will be one complete and perfect entity.

In the meanwhile, you may have revelations from time to time, a few intuitions like lightning, enlightening you momentarily, but not for long, the clouds always reappear. Then again while reading a book, gazing at a beautiful landscape, praying, meditating, you are caught up by some wonderful inspiration and live an important moment of your life. As before it does not last long, all too soon it is over... and so it goes. The life of man is a continual alternation between light and darkness until the day finally comes when he becomes, he *lives* the Spirit. That is, he is born again, into a new Life.

The centre of the personality is the astral body, the body of desire where all the negative ideas and impulses come from. The astral body gives the stimulus, the motive, and the mental body does the arranging and combining that bring us gratification. You must understand this: our desires dictate our behaviour and, although our mind is superior to our desires, capable of putting an end to them and making them listen to reason, it gives in to them. Is it not true that everyone in the world uses the *mind* to carry out the demands of their lower nature? Our learning, our experience, our cultural riches are in the service of something strange and sombre originating in who knows what dark and subterranean places, and the most intelligent, learned, enlightened minds work for forces that are far from clear. That is the sad truth, dear brothers and sisters, if you do not believe me, go and do a little research... you will see.

When the astral body starts working for the intellect, or better still when the intellect starts working for the soul and spirit, that is when perfection becomes possible. It is the purpose of prayer to submit the physical, astral, mental bodies, that is, the lower trinity which thinks, feels and acts for itself only, to the higher Trinity which also thinks, feels and acts, but divinely, for the whole world. The best prayer is to ask the individuality to take over your whole being. As long as the personality is in charge, imposing its will on all your actions, even if the individuality does manage to slip in good advice and blessings from time to time, it cannot remain nor maintain itself, the personality is in command, it has all the power. And that is why nothing works! Yes, the individuality manages to help us from time to time, projecting sparks of light to inspire us, but it does not last... an instant later it disappears. The sad truth is that human beings prefer the personality.

Some people say, "But all that has neither rhyme nor reason, it isn't true, I do not believe it", and go back to living in the personality. Well, people can do as they like! One day they will see how true it is, but in the meanwhile, what a lot of time is lost... better to believe now, right away! Yes, believe, and do everything to let the individuality get the upper hand. This does not mean you become a divinity instantly. No, you will fall and you will pick yourself up... fall and pick yourself up, you will be encouraged and then discouraged... until finally the divine, impersonal consciousness of the individuality moves into its proper place forever.

3

MAN'S TRUE IDENTITY

The greatest of all human errors is the tendency people have to identify with their personality. When they say, I want (money, a car, a girl), I am (ill, well), I have (such an opinion, craving, taste), they believe they are talking about themselves, but they are wrong. It is the personality which wants, thinks, suffers, demands, and when you do not know this, you do everything to satisfy it. People who have never analysed themselves do not know the true nature of the human being, the different planes and stages of evolution, and they identify with the personality, the physical body. The disciple should know that he is something more than the physical body, that all those desires and instincts belong to something that is not himself, for until he knows that, he will not be able to advance along the path to evolution.

The Yoga of self-knowledge is called Jnani-

Yoga. In India, those who want to discover the truth and find out who they really are, practice Jnani-Yoga. It begins with self-analysis: who one is, where one is, why one is. The disciple learns that even if he loses an arm he is still himself, that is, still "me", "I", he is not his arms, nor his legs, nor his stomach, etc..., that is not his real self, he is something more, something above his physical body. Then the disciple examines the realm of emotions and discovers that the feelings he experiences are not himself either, since he can stand back and observe and analyse and control them. His real self is therefore above his emotions. And the same for his thoughts. With this process, little by little he gets to know the real self, the self that is above all else, a most luminous, omniscient, omnipotent, infinite Self which is part of God Himself. After years and years of discipline and spiritual effort (even then it is not given to all disciples), he may finally become one with his higher Self. He sees that the little "me," so uncertain, vulnerable, insignificant, is not the real self, since he can get along without it and discard it like a used envelope, whilst the real Self goes on forever.

Another aspect of this question : a child says, "I," "me," when referring to himself; when he becomes an adult, although he has undergone changes, he goes right on saying, "I" and as an old man he still refers to himself as "I" and "me." The "I" does not change, only the body changes. Then what is the "I"? Man searches for the answer, but does not find it in his physical body, nor in his emotions since his emotions change continually during the course of his life, nor in his thoughts, since his thinking changes quite radically. The one who is permanently "he" is the part that keeps analysing himself all the time until he discovers that he is a part of God Himself. From then on he makes every effort to unite with Him. He comes to the realization that his personality is not eternal, it is not even real, but only a partial and fugitive reflection of his true Self, a mirage, an illusion called "Maya".

The pernicious effect of illusion is that it leads humans along the path of separateness, away from the divine Source which is the real Self, to live in innumerable separate "me"s, all with different desires, emotions, appetites and tendencies. It is not the world that is Maya as some people think, for the world is real, matter is real, as are lies and deception, as is hell. Maya is the personality. It is illusion to think we are separate beings, separate from the life of the universe and separate from the divine Being who is everywhere but whom we can neither feel nor understand because our lower self stands in the way.

A person who begins to rediscover himself through constant study and meditation and, especially, identification with something above the physical body, comes to realize that there is no such thing as separate beings, but only a single Being working through all beings, animating them and manifesting through them unbeknownst to them. Yes, one Being controls and directs all manifestations. Those who understand this truth can no longer be divided against each other, they are incapable of waging war, to them the whole world is one collective being.

An illustration: suppose I put several glasses on this table, all different in colour, form and size. Now, into these glasses I pour perfume, the same perfume in all, with the result that although the containers are different, the *content* is the same essence of perfume. Now, notice that while the glasses remain on the table, with the same form, the essence will on the contrary rise and spread about in the air! The substance of the essence is subtle, delicate and etheric, and mingles with the essence emanating from all the other glasses. This leads us to conclude that above, all essence is *one*.

This picture should make you understand that when we let ourselves be hoodwinked by the personality into seeing nothing but separateness, we are living an illusion, Maya. If we accept to live under this illusion, we will forever be mistaken about reality, our philosophy will never be anything but materialistic, false, incomplete... or let us say our philosophy will be true as long as it concerns matter and form, the outside, the container, but false as soon as it is a question of the contents, that is, of the soul, the spirit, the thoughts and emotions which, blended together, make one.

Now in your imagination picture a group of people sitting round a table who all share a profound love and respect for each other. In appearance, from the materialistic point of view and on the physical plane, they are separate creatures, distinct from each other. That is the limited, erroneous point of view, for between these people currents are circulating, there is a fusion of forces and energies taking place and, because of the fact that love is present, *on another level* they are all one. As long as we are discussing the glasses or our physical bodies, we are confined to certain shapes and forms, but if it is a question of perfume or the inner, subtle life we all have, then there can be no definition or separation, no more contours, no limits, you cannot say, "Here is where the perfume (or life) starts and here is where it stops"! It is impossible, anything that is subtle, mobile, alive, radiant, has no limits.

If you wish to sketch me, my appearance, my face or profile, you are welcome, but will it be me? Has the real "me" an outline? No, for "I" am not the physical body, "I" am the being within who thinks and feels and acts... in an infinitely vaster way than the body you are looking at. And the same is true for you.

What about the sun in the sky with its outline, its form, its definite dimension... how can it reach us across that tremendous distance? So high up, so far away, yet it touches us. It must be because it is able to expand at will. Well, man can do the same thing, yes, by sending his thoughts, which are his rays, through space. When you send a thought toward someone, when you think about him, even if he is thousands of kilometres away, your thought affects him. What is thought? It is our emanations, our projections reaching out into the universe exactly as the quintessence of the sun reaches all the way down to the earth and still further! The rays of the sun are the sun's soul projected into infinite space. Our thoughts are projected by our soul.

And the planets... take the Earth, its liquid part is greater than the solid part; the atmosphere is greater than the liquid part; and the etheric part reaches still further, further than the sun. This is true also for Mercury, Jupiter and Venus, the conclusion being that all the planets are in fact touching, they interpenetrate and impregnate each other, thus forming a unity. Outwardly they are far apart, separate, but inwardly, on the subtle level, they are one. We are like the planets, we come close and touch each other, we are joined and become one through our thoughts and emanations.

That is the true knowledge and science, the true philosophy. He who identifies with his higher Nature finds his true Self, he *knows* himself and becomes conscious of being part of God Himself. It says in the Bible, "Ye are gods." Yes, men are gods. If, unfortunately, they more often seem like animals devouring and killing each other, it is because they have gone too far down into the personality, they live in a region where they are not only limited, but actually cut off from above.

We are all one. That is why, when you think about hurting someone else, you must remember you will be hurting yourself also: you live in that other being and he lives in you. The true morality is to understand that the evil you do to others, you do also to yourself: if someone you love suffers, if he is wounded, you too receive the blow and, if someone is happy and triumphant, that happiness becomes yours as well. It can only be this way however when the philosophy of unity, of love, of universality, penetrates us, that is, the philosophy of "Know thyself." As it is now, it makes us happy when misfortune strikes someone other than ourselves. Alas, yes! We rejoice at the discomfiture of others.

The personality keeps people in that low state of mind; if they do not see it, it is because they identify with the personality instead of identifying with the higher Self. It is exceedingly difficult to stifle certain instincts and desires, but at least be aware that it is not your true Self that has those desires! By becoming detached from yourself, from your personality, you weaken it and then it is easier to create a link with your higher Self and identify with it.

How has man let himself sink so low as not to see the difference between the contents, the quintessence, the soul which is alive, intense, subtle, and that which is lifeless and purely material? To set everything aside for something that is dead! Nothing is more dangerous, for, by dint of concentrating on matter, you come to identify with it and become frozen, immobilized, at the mercy of your enemies. You have to know how to move, to change places, to fly away like birds; if you can fly you are not at the mercy of circumstance. All those who move, who are alive and subtle and mobile, can be inaccessible when they wish, out of reach, no one can capture them, they can always escape to where they are above it all. You say, "Yes, but what about the physical body?" It's true, the physical body is heavy, material, exposed to danger, but the soul... go ahead, try to seize a man's soul, his spirit, his conscience! You can hold the glass in your hand, yes, but not the perfume floating in the air above it!

He who is steeped in matter is at the mercy of other beings who do what they like with him. That is what happens to most humans: they are used by others, moved here or there, put in situations, sent to prison or killed. I draw this conclusion: in order to be above circumstances, above all distress and misfortune, all tragedy, you must glide above events, you must climb ever higher and higher and above all never become crystallized, materialized. Then all human trouble, upheavals, loss, failure, war... nothing will touch you, for you are unseizable, inaccessible, very very high above everything.

To reach that point, you must meditate, using the formula, "I am He," that is, only He exists, I do not exist, I am but a reflection, a shadow. Man is not a separate creature, he is part of God. God alone exists, we are His projection. When we say, "I am He," what we mean is that we do not exist outside of God, we are part of Him, we are near Him until the day we become Him. History has given us proof that creatures have in fact existed who experienced the power, the light, the ecstasy that comes from being able to identify with God. As long as man does not know who he is nor what reality is, he thinks he is his physical body, his emotions and thoughts. He does not know that these are not reality, they are phantasms that make him weak and ill.

4

METHODS OF ESCAPE

All our faults and weaknesses have their roots in the personality. For that reason, there is no use being concerned with your weaknesses, it would take too long, a whole lifetime, to change them, and even then you could never be sure. Far better to do something to alter the roots of the personality, which are what keeps it alive. The main characteristic of the personality is egocentricity: a man ruled by his personality cares only for himself, no one and nothing else counts for him, he thinks himself the centre of the universe, the whole world is there to content him and his wishes, to revolve round him, cater to his whims and love him.

Take lovers: if by any chance the boy forgets to look lovingly at the girl, she is angry, "What? Do that to me! Who does he think he is not to look at me, not to call me or come to see me?" It never occurs to her that he might have been hard at work with no time for himself, that he might be tired. Is she thinking of him, or is that unimportant? And so she reproaches him continuously. The personality has no morals, no ethics, no generosity, no compassion, nothing. The personality wants everything, and, as it never has enough, it remains ungrateful, perpetually irritated not to receive more attention. It is this need to *take* which is at the origin of all greed, rebellion, jealousy, cruelty, vengefulness, egoism.

As long as a man allows his personality to rule him, he will be tormented; someone will always be there refusing to revolve around him, refusing to give him the consideration he believes his due, to recognize his genius, his divinity. All our human misfortunes stem from the way we have overfed our personality: it has become a mountain that bars our way into the Kingdom of God.

Jesus said it was easier for a camel to pass through the eye of a needle than for a rich man to enter the Kingdom of God. I wanted to know why Jesus chose this idea of the camel... and so I went to work to find out why. Yes, that is the kind of thing that amuses me.... I too have my amusements. People are always saying, "Have fun!" and so I do, I carry out their wishes! So I said to myself, what is it that characterizes a camel... and I realized that his astral body is meager, a camel is extremely sober, it crosses the desert without food or drink for long periods at a time; whereas the astral body of a rich man is enormously swollen, he tries to swallow the whole world and everything in it, and that is why he cannot enter the Kingdom of God where only those who have mastered their appetites and conquered their lusts can enter. That is what Jesus meant, otherwise it doesn't make sense... how could the huge body of a camel pass through the eye of a needle, and one man not be able to go through heaven's gate?

The personality has become inflated over the years because of the way man has been brought up, he has been taught to develop the lower nature, the personality and its cravings, until it has become a giant tumour inside him. Let someone say something or touch him and immediately he is provoked, he reacts abnormally, he is sick. He should develop his individuality and forget himself some of the time and think about the situation of others, reasoning kindly, "If he didn't bring me this or that, say this or that, smile this way or that way... perhaps it is because he's tired, or ill, or overworked," instead of tearing himself apart and dreaming up plans of revenge!

If Initiates were in charge of man's education and human behaviour, they would reveal their methods for developing the higher side of human nature, the individuality, the impersonal, disinterested, generous, noble side. That is not the way it is today: people are taught only how to develop and exploit their personality by catering to its every wish, with the result that everyone behaves as though he were the only one on earth, the centre of the universe, and the world should be at his feet. How can people expect to get along and live happily together with that kind of mentality? The basis, the reason behind all the conflict, all the crime, all the trouble in the world is the over-developed personality. Schools and universities have led students in the wrong direction. Let us suppose I were given a certain degree of responsibility in connection with education: I would make a clean sweep and change it entirely, the purpose, direction, and goal of education would change radically and so would the youth of the land! In only a few years' time, everything would be entirely different.

I want to give you an example of the attitude people have. You may think it a bit exaggerated, but nevertheless it is the way the majority think. Here is a couple, man and wife: now watch what happens. Every morning the husband goes off to work, "Goodbye, goodbye, dear...." They kiss each other halfheartedly, distractedly, absorbed in other things. As soon as the door is closed, the wife begins to fret, "How stupid I was to marry that fellow! He is an incapable clumsy good-for-nothing... whereas the couple next door.... Ah, there's a man! He has bought her a new car, she is covered with jewels.... Alas, poor me!" And all day she bewails her fate, "No, no, I simply cannot put up with it any more. When that imbecile comes home tonight, he will hear a thing or two from me!" She spends the day fulminating, filling herself with venom.

Meanwhile the husband is thinking, "Ah, that (I will not repeat the word), why did I have to make the mistake of marrying her? So ordinary, so stupid, so dumb! All she does is go shopping with her stupid dog and have endless conversations with her girl-friends while I have to work here in this infernal noise and racket... to bring *her* money! This is unbearable, it cannot last. When I get home tonight I will give her a piece of my mind...." With so much mutual complaining, how can they do anything when they meet in the evening but tear each other apart? The next day it begins all over again, and so it goes, day after day.

Here is another example: in the morning when it is time to go, this husband and wife embrace tenderly, much more warmly than the other couple and after he goes the wife thinks to herself, "Oh, the poor thing, when I think how much he sacrifices for me! What did he ever see in me to have married me, he who is so noble, so wonderful, so honest! How much love he has! The way he kissed me! He works all day long under terribly difficult conditions with not a minute to breathe and here I am, free to rest or go out or do anything I want! I must cook a wonderful dinner for him tonight." And all day she thinks about him with love and longing and appreciation. This is what makes her a happy wife.

And as he goes off to work he thinks, "What was I thinking of to make this wonderful girl marry me, she has to work so hard cleaning and washing all day, taking care of the children and so on with no time for herself. I can have a drink with my friends and talk things over with them but she, poor darling, has to stay by herself all day and be there to greet the children when they come home. Heaven has blessed me with a lovely wife! I am going to do something for her." And on the way home he picks up some flowers and a little gift to surprise her. All evening they bill and coo happily.

Actually, neither couple is better than the other one, the difference is in their minds, their way of seeing each other. It is the point of view we need to change. To change oneself is practically impossible but it is quite easy to change one's point of view, and then all the rest changes. I want you to realize that the personality and the individuality are two *points of view*.

So, do not consider it essential to obey all the demands of the personality! Even when it has a reason to be discontented or irritated, you must tell the personality, "Listen here, if I go along and react the way you do, I will get into trouble... what if *you* became more reasonable?" This kind of conversation deflates the personality! It must not be allowed to advise you, it should be the other way round, you, the real you, your higher Self, should be the one to give it advice if things are to work out as they should. But no one has any very clear ideas on the subject of how things should be and so everybody does what the personality suggests. This is so, I have seen it even with the most intelligent, learned, literary, scholarly, scientific pundits! They allow themselves to be guided by the personality and think they are the ones to make decisions, but it is really the personality. The personality is very close, like a second skin, but it is not the person himself. Man is his higher Self, the individuality, that is, intelligent, strong, wise, radiant, immortal, infinite, yes, all those things... and more, only he is not yet living in the individuality and identifying with it; he is still sleeping, satisfied to be on the level of the personality, and that is where he is wrong.

As long as you identify with the personality, you will be vulnerable, because it will always be urging you to make demands on others that they are unable to satisfy. Everyone has worries and problems; if your happiness depends on them, on their helping you with your problems, you will never be happy! Someone may help you momentarily, but he may not be around forever. That is why I say to you: if you wait to be loved, appreciated and sought after, you will always be tormented because you are counting on uncertainty. You may be loved for an instant, but who knows what will happen the next instant? You should not count on the love of others. You may obtain it, of course, it may come, it may last forever... if so, make it welcome! But don't count on it. Is what you want happiness? Then do not ask to be loved. Love others, keep on loving them day and night, and you will be happy all the time. Maybe one day you will experience a wonderful love, why not? It may happen, but don't wait for it, don't look for it. For me that solves the problem: I count only on the fact that I love, I *want* to love others, all the others, and, if others do not want to love me, that is their business, they will no doubt be unhappy, but not I, I am overwhelmed with happiness. The question is solved. If you find a better solution, come and see me!

I have made such a thorough study of the personality, I believe I know just about everything now, the way it walks, the way it eats, its laugh, its conversation, its advice... it is a whole world! You too should learn what its gestures are, its language, the way it looks at people, its colours... yes, even its colours. The personality has no radiant colours, it is never luminous except in moments of sexual effervescence when it lights up briefly, but not for long, very soon it is dull again. When it is vexed, its look is so black you can recognize the personality instantly, unmistakably. Of course it can caress and embrace when it wants something; the individuality also caresses and embraces, but the same gesture fills you with poetry, with music... with Heaven! Both like to kiss, but their way of kissing is entirely different... you have probably never noticed. Do you always know when someone is kissing you whether it is his personality or his individuality?

This is a new idea for you: when the personality kisses you, it takes everything from you without a thought for the state it leaves you in, because it has no real feeling for you, it is only seeking to satisfy itself. Whereas the individuality wants to share the abundant love in its heart and soul with you and fills you with beauty, with riches that last for days. To be able to distinguish between the manifestations of the individuality and those of the personality is something you should know about love. It is not easy, for the personality is very good at play-acting, it knows how to fool you. It also knows a great deal about beauty, music, poetry, the dance, all the arts. It is charming, it expresses itself remarkably well, but nevertheless its aim is to devour you. It knows how to look at you with love, to win you, to please you, and everything it does is terribly charming, graceful and beautiful. Yes, but you are devoured in the meantime, caught in the net of the personality. Why is it so charming? The better to devour you! The individuality likewise can be poetic, musical, lovely and fragrant, but the difference is the aim. The aim of the individuality is not to eat you nor to tie you down, but to set you free, to revive you, to help you! The whole point is that: the aim. If you do not know what the aim is, what do you know? When a man gives a present to a girl, does she know why? In appearance it is wonderful, she thinks it is kind of him... but his aim is to take advantage of her.

The personality is far from stupid, on the contrary, it is most erudite, so erudite that it can bring you the moon and the stars in order to convince you not to go on doing good, to cease your spiritual work. No doubt it will succeed in convincing you, because the personality includes scientists and scholars and artists, it is not alone! A whole world exists inside the personality.

Yes, the personality is highly gifted, immensely capable, endowed with many riches... but it is not to be relied upon nor obeyed. On the contrary, it must be dominated.

5

THE SUN SYMBOLIZES THE DIVINE NATURE

If you take the trouble to observe how humans live, you will see that in all fields, personal, social, political, economic, the difficulties come from the fact that most people do everything for their own benefit, not for others. Their interest is purely egotistical, their ideal, their standard, is always to take, for everything begins and ends with *them*: the motive of this civilisation, the point everywhere is to take. People study, work, meet, marry, in order to take from each other, the mind is trained in that direction. Men no longer emanate light, warmth, life, because of their habit of taking. Even in love, a man and woman seek each other only in order to take.

This tendency to acquire, to take, to possess, is the strongest characteristic of the personality. As I told you, the personality is a trinity, a triangle pointing upwards. It corresponds with the trinity of the mind, the heart and the will, but in their lower manifestations, and when it comes up against forces which seem to oppose the realization of its selfish desires and tendencies, it immediately mobilizes all it has, all its mental, emotional and voluntary resources, in order to obtain what it wants.

The higher Self, on the contrary, wants only to enlighten, to radiate light, to give, to help, to sustain others, it is always trying to project something of itself, it emanates generosity and self-abnegation. That is why it does not hide its possessions and is not irritated when someone wants to take from it, on the contrary, it is happy to be able to give people what they need: food and drink and light. The individuality also is a trinity of the mind, the heart and the will, but here the desire of the mind, or intelligence, is to shine, the desire of the heart is to shed warmth, and the desire of the will is to revive people, animate them and set them free.

The fundamental virtue of the higher Nature is to give. That is what virtue is: a radiance, a projection of the self from the centre to the periphery, a need for sacrifice, for the giving of self, like the sun which gives and gives. The personality is like the earth in that it does nothing but take. The earth contributes nothing to the cosmos, the sun does. The inhabitants of Jupiter or Saturn looking through their telescopes can see how feeble a light this poor little globe emanates, but even that light is not its own. The earth does not produce much light because it is still too selfish: egoism does not project light! Light comes from inside the Self, Light is the expression of love and abnegation.

The sun is the illustration of the desire to *give,* the earth is the illustration of the desire to *take*. This does not mean that the earth gives nothing... it takes what it receives and produces flowers, plants and fruit... but always for itself. Do the stars and planets benefit from the earth's flowers and fruit? No, they belong to the earth and to earth-children (which is the same thing), whereas the sun sends what it produces far out in space so that as many creatures as possible can profit. There are two laws, the law of absorption (acquisition), and the law of emission (radiation). The sun is the perfect example of the law of emission.

When you watch the sun rise each morning, you are seeing the perfect example of generosity, the giving of the self, the sublime manifestation of the individuality, the Spirit, the Divine. The trouble is that if no one explains what is actually occurring and how to interpret it, you will keep looking and looking but nothing will stop you from following the law of the earth, the personality: you will go on taking. Once you understand what the sunrise really is, then you will sense the power, grandeur and immensity of the act of giving, you will want to change yourself and everything inside you, rejoicing because day by day you can become a little more like the sun.

Yes, you must learn to give as the sun gives, and not wait for a reward any more than the sun does. People make little sacrifices from time to time and then wait for thanks in return, a little praise, a compliment. You think this is only normal, but the rules of the earth are not the same as the rules of the sun.

Egoism always has a pernicious effect on man. When you keep everything you receive for yourself alone, certain canals inside you become blocked; you know what happens when a spring dries up: fermentation, nauseating odours, vermin accumulate, all because the spring stopped flowing! The same thing happens inside us, the personality becomes like stagnant water.

On the other hand there is nothing as capable, inventive or resourceful as the personality: in order to eat, in order to *have*, it has had to learn to get along on its own and it does very well... yes, it is active, prompt, decisive, violent even,in getting its own way. The individuality is neither as dynamic nor as resourceful; the remarkable thing about the individuality is that it flows and keeps on flowing, spreading light and vitality and watering and fertilizing everything along its path. The individuality is a source, a spring, and if it is allowed to manifest itself, this abundance, this love and kindness, this purity and light and generosity fill the person entirely, he feels cleansed and light and radiant.

You see, it is easy to evolve! "What do you mean, easy!" you exclaim. "For years and years I have been trying with no success!" It is because you have not done the essential, you are not applying the law of giving, of sacrifice. What you do is for *you*, to enrich yourself, even when you read, when you study, still you are taking. Only when you begin to distribute to others all that you have learned in books, in life, in all you have done and all you are doing, will you be able to change and progress. People work, naturally, but they work in order to acquire, they develop themselves in order to gain more power, to spread their tentacles all over the world like branch offices of a supermarket... they do not work to *give*.

Jesus touched on this question. He did not explain what he meant nor use these words, but if you interpret the Gospels correctly, you will see that he knew the importance of detachment from worldly things.

"The rich young man asked Jesus, Good

Master, what good thing shall I do that I may have eternal life? Jesus answered, Why callest thou me good? There is none good but one, that is, God: but if thou wilt enter into life, keep the commandments. The young man asked, Which? And Jesus answered, Thou shalt do no murder, Thou shalt not commit adultery, Thou shalt not steal, Thou shalt not bear false witness, Honour thy father and thy mother and, Thou shalt love thy neighbour as thy self. The young man said, All these things have I kept from my youth up, what lack I yet? Jesus said, If thou wilt be perfect, go and sell that thou hast, and give to the poor, and thou shalt have treasure in Heaven, and come and follow me. But when the young man heard that saying he went away sorrowful, for he had great possessions. Then said Jesus unto his disciples, Verily I say unto you, That a rich man shall hardly enter into the Kingdom of Heaven. And again I say unto you, It is easier for a camel to go through the eye of a needle than for a rich man to enter into the Kingdom of Heaven."

The rich young man was not ready to divest himself of his earthly possessions, and he did not follow Jesus. The fact that Jesus asked such a thing shows that he knew the importance of the law of giving and taking. Why give? To become free, to do what the sun does and to become like it! The same idea in a different form. From now on, if you have understood me, you will look at the sun in a new way and you will begin to change. Everything depends on comprehension, on the way of seeing things. Only by understanding, by true and deep comprehension, is man able to release the divine currents within him... when he does, he becomes transformed into a sun himself, giving as the sun gives. He finds he is richer and has never had so much to give, never been so clear and lucid, so strong and powerful.

Jesus said, "And if any man will sue thee at the law and take away thy coat, let him have thy cloke also." Why? To do as the sun does. Obviously Jesus did not *say* it was in order to resemble the sun, but the idea is the same: to become so powerful inside that you are beyond fear. Fear must be overcome. It says in the Gospels, "The Kingdom of God is for the courageous." It is the personality which fears, never the individuality. The personality fears for itself because it is isolated, poor, vulnerable, that is why it always tries to take, to amass things, to insure its security. When one is afraid, it is not love that one manifests. Love is incompatible with fear; where love is, fear disappears. The personality in the grip of fear is at its most ignoble.

Now I want to give you the spiritual interpretation of the law of Newton. Newton discovered the existence of universal attraction and put it into a formula: "The planets move as if attracted by the sun in direct proportion to their mass and inversely proportional to the square of their distance from the sun." Thus attraction is in proportion to the mass of bodies and inversely proportional to their distance. Later, physicists made this experiment: they weighed an object at the pole and at the equator, and they saw that at the equator the object weighed less than at the pole. Why? Because of the fact that the earth is slightly flatter at the poles, making the distance less to the equator. Attraction is then greater at the pole and the object is heavier there. But if the object goes away from the earth, there comes a moment when it will no longer be subject to the earth's attraction and will therefore be weightless. Let us now suppose it enters into the solar field of attraction: the same law goes into effect, it will be attracted by the sun. Thus, this same object which was attracted by the earth, we now see moving towards the sun, drawn by the sun until it is completely absorbed.

It is the same for the human being, situated as he is somewhere between the earth and the sun, between the personality and the individuality: if he remains close to the earth, his personality keeps its hold on him and he weighs heavily. But the further away he goes, the less power the personality has over him... until the moment when he moves toward the sun, toward his higher Self, his individuality, when it has no more power over him at all! It is the same law, but astronomers are too busy with the physical plane to discover that this law exists also on the spiritual plane.

To move about easily in space, man must cut certain bonds, his dependence on certain things: to do that he must learn to give. The way to reach detachment is by divesting oneself, sacrificing oneself, renouncing oneself, *giving* oneself. Thus by giving, you remove yourself further and further from the earth, until you are seized by the sun and absorbed into it.

If now after all these explanations you have no desire to embrace the philosophy of the individuality, it means the personality has a firm hold on you... too firm a hold. For years, for millenniums, the personality has been handed down from family to family through all kinds of philosophies, until it has become so much a part of us that no matter what we hear we will go on doing what the personality advises. We say, "We are very well as we are, thank you, and if we must go through trouble and sorrow, what do you expect? That's life!" And so we accept our suffering, our slavery, we have no hope of anything better.

This new philosophy will not easily be accepted by those who are caught in the grip of the personality and have no taste for a higher existence, for something more beautiful and poetic. You say, "But then, if you know in advance that humans will not follow you, why do you go on talking to them?" Because I also know that some people will escape and no longer be prisoners of the personality: I speak for them. I hope that some of you will manage to extract yourselves from the vicious circle of the personality and be attracted to the divine world. As for the others, I have no illusion. After many disasters, many lessons... in a few incarnations from now, perhaps they too will extract themselves from the claws of the personality.

The personality first appeared during the animal reign (animals also have a higher Nature, but it is dormant). Now it is the higher Nature that is beginning to manifest itself in humans, begging to be allowed to live in us and reign over us as with the Initiates. That is the ideal we should all have: to make the divine Nature welcome! The sun is the symbol of this ideal, which is why Initiates adopted it as their model. Someone will say, "But the sun is not human!" Perhaps not, but it does more than humans do! Is it not better to be like a creature whose faculties far surpass human faculties, than to remain feeble, insignificant, cruel, mediocre, selfish and ignorant as men are?

Suppose the sun *is* no more than metal or stone in fusion, what of it? As long as it manifests qualities that are superior to human qualities, as long as it distributes light, heat, and life, I will go toward it without wondering what it is, human, stone or metal. If I see that its qualities and virtues far surpass man's qualities and virtues, then I want to go toward it, I know that if I am near it I will grow more intelligent, I will be exalted, I will become healed. Whereas humans tend to make one ill and unhappy. Someone will say, "My God, what nonsense! Now he is endowing the sun with intelligence and qualities!" Why not? I am not the only one, the example was set by many great Beings before me.

Another argument in favour of the sun: when you are looking at someone, how can you tell what he thinks and what action he is planning? If his face is somber, sinister, menacing, you can be sure he is planning some criminal act. Nature has so arranged things that when a man is planning something criminal, his face darkens, he stops radiating; when he is planning to do some good for the entire world, his face clears, he becomes radiant. Could we not draw a fantastic conclusion from this observation? Why does the sun shine, what makes the face of the sun always luminous, always radiant? It is because the sun is ceaselessly thinking good things, wonderful things! Its light is proportional to the grandeur of its good thoughts, good feelings, abundant love and knowledge. Had you ever thought of that? The sun points the way, telling us to give, to enlighten others, to vivify creatures wherever we go. But people are too far removed from this way of thinking, this Science, to allow themselves to be persuaded, they say, "Very poetic, a pretty thought," but they will not change anything.

How many things still to reveal! For the moment much is still unclear in your minds because you have not gone deeply enough into the science of symbols and analogies. But patience! It will all come clear in a little while.

6

PUT THE PERSONALITY TO WORK

If you observe the personality you see that it cannot hide or disguise itself, for its attitude and manner, its way of giving advice at the top of its voice and demanding attention at all times, are unmistakable. Once familiar with its tricks, you are no longer fooled but this requires constant vigilance, you must be willing to study and analyse the methods of the personality if you are ever to dominate it.

For instance, you make a decision to give up something it enjoys, but there it is, waiting for you at the first turn, ready to persuade you to look at the situation in another light. You are convinced and give in! It is hard to decide to give up something you are used to... tobacco, wine, women, money... and the personality knows this, it knows exactly what to say and do to confuse the issue, "Well! Given up drinking have you? A magnificent thing to do! It calls for a celebration!" And off you go to the nearest pub, which is precisely what you have determined not to do. The personality is a wily one!

I am not saying the personality should be done away with completely. No, like a rich old lady it holds the keys to the safe, to the larder, the cupboards; it owns stocks and bonds, bars of gold and a store of treasures still in their crude state, that is, instincts, appetites, passions, desires. The personality is strong and powerful, extremely able, talented, resourceful, but the trouble is, it wants everything to revolve round it. For all its egocentricity it must not be despised, for it is the personality that preserves us and increases our possessions. Again, the trouble is that it lacks honesty, it has no conscience, no morality or ethics, no sense of fair play, no kindness or generosity... it is entirely selfish!

The personality is the reservoir of our potential, it is a necessary part of us... the point is, we must be more intelligent than it is, we must make it submit and obey instead of being subservient to it. The best way is to put it to work to realize, not *its* ideas but *ours.* No one, you can be sure, no one, is as capable as the personality at working things out, as a worker it is unique; the thing I envy most is its indefatigability: you can say what you like about the rest, but it is a great quality to be tireless. Truants and criminals are indefatigable, their minds are forever working on diabolical projects... but kind people, nice, good souls, are always tired! They have no great zest for stealing, no desire for revenge or murder, no great ambition... what else is there? Earning a living, fulfilling their marital duties, bringing up their children and feeding the chickens... you can't expect more from them. The personality does a tremendous amount of work in every direction but unless you keep it under control, you will be the one doing the work!

The personality has great power and can be enormously useful to you once you learn to use it, as man finally learned to use the forces of Nature. Before man put electricity, water and air to work for him, he was their victim; now they perform miracles for him! Why shouldn't it be the same for the natural forces within? If the disciple learns how to harness those forces when they threaten to annihilate him, and put them to work, he will see what an extraordinarily clever engineer the personality is... he will have waterworks, electric currents, windmills, dams and all kinds of great works inside! This is what a disciple learns from Initiatic Science.

You see what a lot of changes there are to make, what a lot there is to learn. How to use vanity, for instance, and anger, and sexual energy. I have discovered how to sit back and let my vanity do all the work, without my vanity I could not get half as much done, I put it to work and let it move mountains while I twirl my thumbs! Why get rid of vanity? On the contrary, I feed it and pat it and make it work for me.... I never claimed to be free of vanity, I am proud of what it does for me, and the same for the other forces... I keep them busy, hard at work. The point is, the forces are not there in us to be either fought against or submitted to: they are there to do the work.

An Initiate has as much personality as anyone else, but he keeps it rationed, he gives it just enough nourishment to save it from starving to death, but never does he give in to its demands, he is always in control. Not like the signs you see in some houses that say, "I am the master here but my wife gives the orders!" The Initiate's sign reads, "I am the master here and the personality is my obedient servant." He will not kill his personality as the saintly hermits and ascetics of the past did... believing they were meant to live in filth, in penitence and privation and consequently the personality was wasted, of no use to them whatsoever.

I advise you to take care of the personality, watch over it and feed it, but do not allow it to have its way. Do you leave a servant without food or lodging? You see to it that he is taken care of, but you do not ask him to run your affairs or issue orders. I know of cases where the servant became so important she took over the role of mistress of the house from her boss... her delicious dishes were so indispensable to him that he could not bear to be without her and married her. The servant became the mistress by catering to her master's appetites! Read the biographies of some of the world's great leaders and you will see how true this is. I am not suggesting that the servant, the personality, be crushed or done away with, but rather tamed and domesticated, its freedom limited. If not, in your absence it will take advantage of its freedom to invite the neighbours in and when you come back, the cupboard will be bare, the bottles empty! Yes, when the mind is absent, the personality seizes the opportunity to invite its friends on the astral plane, that is, all your lower thoughts and feelings come and celebrate your departure by eating your best food, drinking your best wine and ransacking the house!

In order not to be dominated by the personality, the disciple must learn to assert his control over it. As I said, this is difficult to do because the personality is clever, it knows how to assume and retain its place as ruler, as mistress of the house, as commander-in-chief, and it will not give up easily. Relax your vigilance, show a little confusion and, even if you succeed in gaining the upper hand momentarily, it is always waiting to jump back in and put you at its mercy.

Two countries fight a war against each other until one or the other finally wins; the conquered country then has to relinquish some of its territory, submit to occupation by the enemy, pay enormous taxes and levies, etc... but the triumph is short-lived, supremacy is never permanent, never conclusive. A conquered nation always has fanatical patriots who refuse to accept defeat, rebels who work underground secretly plotting their country's liberation. Behind the scenes, in silent darkness, the mines are laid and the day the enemy sits back proudly, sure of himself and resting on his laurels, he is taken by surprise and the situation is once again reversed. We have seen this phenomenon again and again in the political and economic histories of the peoples of the world... as well as in our own lives.

What I am trying to say is that the same thing is true of the inner life, the spiritual life: we will never be able to subjugate the personality entirely, as long as we live it will go on working even if it has to go underground. It will never give up. For it to remain submissive and obedient, you have to be armed to the teeth and vigilant at all times, and this is exhausting, even saints and Initiates grew tired and were forced to let go... this is just what the personality is waiting for. Nothing is as persistent as the personality! You all know what wheat-grass is... well, the personality is a form of wheat-grass.

What can be done about it? We must realize that by ourselves, alone, we are not well enough equipped to fight against evil; evil is extremely well-armed, it has an arsenal that puts our forces to shame. We must therefore look for an ally and join forces to make the battle less unequal. What do nations do when they are attacked? They ask other nations to be their allies. Man has always known instinctively that he must have help from others when he is in danger, alone he is too vulnerable. Why not realize that evil has a great many resources, great knowledge, great cunning and power, and that we will never be able to conquer it by ourselves. The solution is for us to link ourselves with God, with celestial Beings, Archangels and Divinities, and ask them, entreat them, beg them to help us win the battle. Then we become spectators, watching Heaven carry off the victory and the enemy flee! Heaven, that is, our divine Self, has the power and means to cope with evil, but we, who are we to oppose the powers of evil?

Never try to destroy your personality... not only will you not be able to destroy it, but you will be the one to be destroyed. Instead, link yourself with Heaven, and then handle the personality with the absolute conviction that you are its master. It will have to obey you and step down in favour of the individuality. You should know however, that even if you succeed in making the personality submit to the individuality, it does not mean it will disappear entirely. No, it will keep its roots in the physical body, the last refuge of the personality. Even if no trace of selfish desire remains in the astral body, still the personality will control the physical body and it is right that it should, for if it disappeared entirely from the physical plane, the individuality would not be able to manifest itself. On the psychic plane the personality is replaced once and for all, but never as far as the physical plane is concerned. The replacement can be compared to new personnel in administrations, banks and universities: the buildings do not change, everything continues to function as before, but from time to time certain people are replaced.

For your better understanding, I will repeat what I have told you about the memory. The cells of the physical body are renewed supposedly every seven years: then why do we go right on making the same mistakes, doing the same stupid things and having the same old weaknesses and vices? It would be absolutely inexplicable if we did not know that when the system takes on new material to replace the used material, one thing remains unchangeable: it is the cell's memory. A new cell takes the place of the old one but goes right on working exactly as the old one did.

In offices and factories, when the older employees retire, they are replaced by young ones who go on doing the same work. This is what I mean by memory: the new ones inherit the traditional methods but the objectives remain the same and there is no interruption of the work. Human beings go on making the same mistakes from generation to generation because of the *memory* of the cells. The particles, the cells are new, but they make the same gestures, speak the same way, want the same things and do the same things as always. If you were to ask God to let your personality be replaced by the individuality, you would then affect the memory of the cells, you would change the recorded habits and clichés, the old ways would be replaced by a new and better behaviour.

What I am saying here is terribly important. Even if you do manage to control your personality, alone you will not be able to make it obey you or carry out your more evolved plans and projects... it may try, but it cannot, because it has not yet formed the clichés, it has no memory. Even if it wants to accept the new imprints, it has no room for them because of the old imprints, and so it sits back, waiting for the moment to assert itself again. Whereas if you invite your higher Self to take possession of you, the old habits, the old memory will be erased and then... it will no longer be the personality but the individuality that does the work! The physical plane (stomach, lungs, brain, etc...) still exists of course, but in an entirely renovated interior!

St. Paul said, "I am crucified with Christ; nevertheless I live, yet not I, but Christ liveth in me...." Christ manifested himself through the man called Paul, that is, through his personality. When the personality is replaced, the contents alone are changed... as when you stuff dead animals: everything is removed from their insides, but they still retain the form of a bear or lion, hawk or eagle. When the individuality comes to dwell in you, you will not change your form, you will still seem like the same person everyone knows, but your innermost memory will have been replaced, in your heart of hearts you will be different. Those who know you will gradually realize that you emanate a new element. That is the wondrous thing, you are the same person but at the same time you are completely different!

And so, dear brothers and sisters, here you must be resigned to hearing the same boring subject of the personality and the individuality: after all, this knowledge will give you the possibility of transforming your existence! I know you prefer to hear other things, such as the magic secrets of the Kabbala. Well, no, you are stuck with someone who came for the express purpose of annoying mankind: I am asking you to work on your *character*, to change your way of living. Of course it is displeasing to you, but try not to be too angry with me, a little if you must, but not too much! I have been charged with this mission to teach, and I must do it. I could chat for hours on all kinds of other subjects, but how would that change your character, your life? I do not believe it would.

Therefore, drop all the things that will not transform your existence and apply yourselves more and more to improving the way you live. When you do that, all the rest, the wisdom, the learning, will come of its own accord. If you do not, this is what will happen: you will have read a great many books, you will have acquired information which will last a while, a few years maybe, after which it will be gone, forgotten! Why? Because you lived your life in such a way that you forgot everything you learned. Is it worth spending so much time acquiring an education that disappears in no time? If you improve your life, your way of living, the memory deep inside you will awaken and bring back everything you learned over the centuries, during all your reincarnations. You will have read nothing at all yet you will know everything! That is the real memory. Make a note of this and never forget it: the person who knows how to live divinely attracts the wisdom of the ages, it enters inside and even shows on the surface. He has obtained true wisdom.

7

PERFECTION COMES WITH THE HIGHER SELF

I

Take a tree, for instance: in studying it you see that the roots, trunk and branches are similar to man's personality or lower self, whereas the leaves, blossoms and fruit correspond to his individuality or higher Self. The personality is the physical, material side which acts as a support, a conductor; the individuality provides the spiritual element, the spirit or life behind all manifestation. Both are necessary, we cannot do without either one.

As the tree grows taller and taller, its roots sink deeper and deeper into the ground, the trunk thickens, the branches spread wide and the tree reaches high into the sky. The roots, trunk and branches have the function of supporting the leaves, blossoms and fruit, they are there permanently; the leaves, blossoms and fruit come and go according to the seasons. The personality, that is, our physical, astral and mental bodies, has the same role, it is our permanent mainstay and support, whereas the individuality, the spiritual nature which is our inspiration, joy and happiness, comes to us intermittently from the Causal, Buddhic and Atmic bodies.

You can do anything you wish with man, feed him to make him strong, instruct him to make him learned, but his personality will still be the same, the personality never changes because it is human nature and human nature does not change (if it did it would no longer be human nature). For the human tree to bear fruit, the divine nature must be allowed to manifest itself. The Scriptures say, "...every good tree bringeth forth good fruit, but a corrupt tree bringeth forth evil fruit. Every tree that bringeth not forth good fruit is hewn down and cast into the fire. Wherefore by their fruits ye shall know them." The personality and the individuality! "Perhaps," you say, "but the alchemists were able to transform lead into gold, were they not?" No, there you are mistaken. They did not transform lead or any other metal into gold, the metal was made to disappear, and the gold *replaced* it. In the same way, the personality will never be divine, the best it can do is disappear and leave room for the individuality to manifest in its place. What will happen? The physical, astral and mental bodies (which make up the personality) will disappear and eventually the higher bodies will manifest themselves in all their glory. The personality is only a receptacle: however you may try to improve it, it cannot change its egocentric nature... when it does, it will no longer be the personality! Never count on the personality to improve! Use it, put it to work, make it step down in favour of the individuality or higher Self, the infinite and omnipotent Spirit. People think when they are in a negative frame of mind that their personality has become worse... and when they are in good spirits, that their personality has improved. They are wrong. The lower nature never improves, the higher Nature has simply been given the right conditions, the chance to manifest itself. But never for very long... again the personality grabs the controls and, because it is not equipped to govern, you are in a dreadful state of confusion! And so on and on. What you must understand is that what we call the "I" is not the one who is subject to these variations, going from better to worse, no, the "I" does not change, but two absolutely different natures expressing themselves alternately through the "I".

The individuality is never negative, somber or selfish, if you have a tendency in that direction, it shows that the personality dominates in you over the individuality. Nor does the same nature pass from one state to another: good cannot become evil, and evil cannot become good, each is what it is for all eternity.

When a person does some wonderful deed, it is because he has succeeded in getting away from the personality for a moment. Later, when everything seems exactly as it was, he identifies with the personality and laments, "I am condemned to remain the same forever!" No. Why does he identify himself with his personality? He has only to identify with the individuality and he will keep doing wonderful things all the time! His error is that he does not always remain on the level that allowed him to do those wonderful things; after praying and meditating, after contemplating the heavens and experiencing rapture and ecstasy, why must he come back down to the level of the lower self? That is why he thinks, "I am always the same! I am not advancing! I never improve at all." What about the rapture and ecstasy he experienced, who achieved all those extraordinary things? In any case not his lower self! You see how many things are not yet clear in your heads.

Let us say you have just been meditating and praying earnestly, you are bathed in light and far removed from the world of passion and lust... just then a pretty girl appears and you react as usual. "But why?" you say to yourself, "I was so far from all that while I was meditating and praying!" Yes, when you were in the individuality you were detached from "all that" but when you came back down into the personality (which in the meanwhile was alert and waiting) it manifested itself as usual. If you walk by a restaurant when you have not eaten for several days, the smell of food is very appetizing!

In times of peace, people are more or less amiable, smiling and kind, but when war breaks out, how destructive they become! Is it they who change? No, it is one of the two natures manifesting through them according to what the conditions are. Take a young girl: at the start she is absolutely innocent, pure and virginal, but put her down in certain conditions and you will see what she is capable of! Yes, the personality always eventually demands its rights.

If you have understood what I told you today, it will be most enlightening for you. Man has always thought he could change evil, but he cannot, it is a question of one or the other. When good manifests itself, evil disappears, it fades away, but if good loses its grip for a single instant, you will see to what extent evil is still there. Evil is not eternal, not everlasting as good is, but it can be transformed only by a cosmic decree, Cosmic Intelligence alone can decide when and how to do it. In the meanwhile, evil is fulfilling its mission, which is to teach humans a lesson. The trouble is, humans fail to discern what the Cosmic plan is. They think evil will exist eternally and that good and evil will go on fighting each other forever. They think evil is as powerful as God, that it opposes Him, and that He is dependent on humans (such as knights and crusaders) for help in His fight against the Devil!

Evil is not meant to exist forever, it exists now because God has given it the right to exist, evil depends on God and when He gives the signal, it will disappear. God is eternal, evil is temporary. Human beings lack the power to make it disappear, our weakness, our fear, our ignorance prevent us. God alone has power over evil. That is why we must beg the divine Self to take over and manifest through us so that the evil in us will be replaced by good. I know this idea is not easy to accept but, with the help of meditation and prayer, the light will come, our friends in the invisible world will see to it that we are helped.

No exercise, no method, no yoga, will ever be enough to change the lower nature. The brute matter it is made of is too firmly rooted underground, too close to the lower entities and forces which feed it and encourage it to be egocentric, variable, cruel, gross, unfaithful. The individuality has its roots in the higher regions close to God, and when we identify with it, we identify with heaven. Heaven takes possession of us little by little and we are able to work miracles!

The goal of all spiritual exercise is to help the individuality install itself in us. However, no matter how long we meditate, how many years we devote to prayer and sacrifice and effort to change, we remain the same, that is... but I prefer not to enumerate all that comes under the heading of the personality. We accomplish wonderful things at times, yet we remain the same, with the same weaknesses, the same foibles, bad habits and vices, the same sadness. Why? Because the personality has not really disappeared. All that you have been able to accomplish, all the successes you have had, were the result of your letting the individuality manifest itself *at that time*, but, as you continue to live your life according to the wishes of the personality, always identifying with it, you think there is no change in you, and you say, "How sad! I am still the same." For thirty, forty or more years, you have done everything to change, yet you are always the same! This is no cause for dismay, you must simply tell yourself, "I have not succeeded in conquering my personality, but I know why.

It is because I have not let the divine Nature rule me, and that is the only way I can change, really change."

If you decide to change your attitude, you will be transformed. Yes, on condition you give absolute supremacy to the individuality, not just a minute now and then to say a few words or create something beautiful, only to be chased away immediately by the personality. You may succeed in doing some wonderful, splendid things now and then under the inspiration of the individuality, but you will still be capable of doing evil, you will not be free.

Everything man has ever done that was good, creative and useful, was not the result of his or anyone else's efforts but of something divine that came and manifested through him. None of the world's great artistic, poetic, mystic creations were inspired by the personality, all it does is provide the physical material. Everything beautiful comes from above where the higher Nature dwells.

When the personality has been made to step down, when we become "dead unto our lower nature," a higher Being will come and live in us. Human beings, at the moment in the middle somewhere between the two natures, will then be "dead unto" the personality and "alive unto" the individuality. What is the "I," what are "we"? It is a mystery. We are neither the personality nor the individuality, we are something beyond them. But do not think you can learn what constitutes the human being, who and what you are, in one easy lesson! Impossible, it is too great, too profound a mystery, the greatest of all mysteries.

II

Have you noticed that most humans, including the most learned and cultured people, obey their personality almost exclusively? Without realizing it, they devote their most noble attributes, their high intelligence and superior reasoning powers, their sensitivity, to the gratification of their lowest needs and desires, without realizing that those are the very faculties that should be working to realize the ideals of the higher Self.

The Kingdom of God will never come on earth until mankind mobilizes the forces of the higher Nature and puts them to work to realize that goal. But that is precisely where human beings are not enlightened and all their energies, even those of the soul and spirit, are used to satisfy their worst side. The extraordinary thing is that the more they try to satisfy that side, the more keenly they feel the void, the dissatisfaction. The lower nature may be sated but the other nature is famished, it suffers from lack of nourishment and asks, "What about me, is there nothing for me?" That is what creates your feeling of dissatisfaction and emptiness.

No other era has developed the opportunities as much as this one for contenting, pampering the personality, and yet never have men been less satisfied. In the past they got along with very little; today they have everything they could possibly want, and that is why they are perpetually unhappy, empty, unbalanced. All technology, all inventions, are made to work for the lower nature, which is so overfed it vomits.... Why do we not understand that there are other needs to be satisfied? In this twentieth century, the century of light supposedly, people are blind to the essential! The more they are given, the more they lack. Like the story of the husband who gives his wife everything, clothing, jewels, cars, villas, but forgets the essential: love. And so, finding herself unloved and unhappy, one day she elopes with the chauffeur. No doubt he gave her the one element she was lacking, and she gladly gave up everything! As long as you do not know enough to give the one you love the subtle nourishment his soul and spirit require, no matter what you do for him you will have a surprise one day: he will leave you for someone else.

A wife comes and tells me, "I did everything

for my husband, I surrounded him with love and affection, I tried to satisfy all his wishes and desires, and... he left me!" I answer, "Well, maybe that was the trouble. Who did he leave you for?" "A girl who is cold as ice, practically frozen...." "Well, that's it, you were too warm, he has gone to cool off!" And it's true, many women do everything to content their husband's personality, his stomach and sex, but are not able to awaken him or inspire him with a higher form of love... who is to blame the poor thing for looking elsewhere? I know also that some husbands are gross and vulgar people, but that is another subject. Men and women should all recognize this truth : if they nourish the personality of their partner to the exclusion of everything else, they will always meet with disappointment and disillusionment, for the personality is unfaithful and ungrateful, it forgets what is done for it. What we should do is to awaken and stimulate the higher Nature in everyone else, especially those who are close to us, that is what will bring them happiness.

My principle is *not* to satisfy your personality. You do not like that, it makes you angry. Too bad. I am here to feed your soul, your spirit, the divine Nature which is lying inanimate in some corner because you neglect it... and always have. But you, you always want me to pamper the personality with flattery and compliments.... Well no, that would not do anything for you or your evolution. On the other hand, if I do something about your individuality, you will be enriched and make great strides ahead. For centuries, millenniums, you will work and work, and then, one day, you will come and find me among the stars to thank me... the individuality knows how to be loyal and grateful, you see!

You must know that the only interesting thing as far as I am concerned is your individuality, your spirit. I am working in order to liberate you and even if it annoys you I will go on doing it, saying to myself, "One day they will understand and stop being annoyed!"

I gave you the image of the tree to explain the nature and role of the personality in relation to the individuality, but there are other ways of illustrating it. Take a hose: you can pour dirty or clean water through it, or petrol, or any other liquid... the hose will always remain a hose, no matter how precious the liquid that passes through it is. Or take a loud-speaker: the loud-speaker itself does not change with each different voice, each strain of music that it emits. It is the same way for the personality: through its loud-speaker it may be the individuality that manifests itself... but beware of thinking, even when the personality is at its best, that it has improved... no, it is your higher Nature, the individuality, which is manifesting itself at that particular moment, making it appear as though the personality had improved. As with the loudspeaker, paint it another colour, deck it with ornaments, nothing changes it basically. Someone's physical appearance can be altered by surgery, but not his personality, the personality will always be the same, self-centred, unstable, ignorant, willful, egotistical. A man who allows the individuality, the Spirit, his higher Self or divine side to manifest, may seem to have changed, but should the individuality be pushed aside, then the personality will reappear in all the error of its ways. Are you beginning to understand this now?

"We", our conscious self, caught somewhere between the personality and the individuality, are responsible for the manifestations of each one. If it is the individuality we wish to summon, it will come willingly; otherwise it is the personality that manifests itself. You say, "But then, we, who are we?" A screen, we are a screen on which different forms are projected... ugly, beautiful, dark, luminous, all kinds of forms. What should we do? If you want to be on the right path, you must consciously and continually evoke the presence of the higher Self.

Of course, finding the right path does not necessarily mean that everything will be perfect from then on. People decide to change their lives and start to live the divine life: immediately they are plunged in trouble and difficulty of all kinds, as though they had aroused it in themselves! It requires a great deal of patience, it is a stage to go through, a fermentation that must occur inside, the same as in alchemy. In alchemy, the first result or phenomenon obtained is fermentation, whatever the matter is, it becomes dark, it ferments and dies... and then it resuscitates! That is what happens to those who decide to begin the work. It is a necessary stage before the higher Nature can come and manifest itself in us. When I see someone in fermentation I rejoice, I say to myself, "That one is going to find the philosopher's stone that will transmute his metal into gold!"

It will help you to understand if I take the example of the human system: suppose you accumulate a vast amount of poison as a result of leading a disordered life: it does not stop you from eating, drinking, working, and so on... for years you go about carrying this illness, this death hidden within which does not declare itself openly, preferring to hide because it knows that as soon as it appears it will be hunted down, there will be doctors, pills, medicine, surgery...

until it is expurgated. So it prefers to say nothing, and continues to undermine your health in secret. But as soon as you begin to follow certain rules, to practice the exercises that purify you, everything inside starts to come out and the result is fever and soreness, stiffness, colic, headache! Everything is turned upside down when the system takes its courage in both hands and says, "The time has come to chase away all these spongers, these miscreants who live at our expense," and makes every effort to shake them off. It is the beginning of your combat against the undesirables installed in you, the combat that will lead to liberation.

Let us come back to the image of the tree because it is the one that provides us with the best idea of the way the personality and the individuality function. When, each Spring, the tree begins to manifest its leaves, blossoms and fruit, it is the individuality coming to life! Why are the leaves, blossoms and fruit not always in evidence? They come and go (like poetic inspirations that bring light to us from time to time, and then abandon us again to our prose), whereas the roots, trunk and branches, the personality, is always there. The personality can grow and become tall and thick but it will always be the personality, the roots (sex and stomach), the trunk (lungs and thorax) and the branches (the brain).

All we need do to make the change occur, is to bring the Spirit down, to be a conductor as it passes through us, and then yes, there will be changes, extraordinary changes! Just as the tree blossoms out into leaves and fruit (to our great joy), so when man lets the current of the individuality pass through him, it acts as a blessing that affects all around him. Like the tree, man grows tall and strong... but unless the divine energy, the spiritual force, passes through him, his personality will keep him bare and sterile as a tree in winter.

Let us look at the similarities between the tree and man in connection with his different bodies: the roots correspond to his physical body, the trunk to his astral body, and the branches to his mental body. The three bodies, physical, astral and mental, form the lower trinity of the personality. They are what cause man to act, to feel and to think, but only in the lower regions. The Causal body is similar to the leaves, the Buddhic body to the blossoms, and the Atmic body to the fruit of the tree. They are the higher trinity of the individuality, thanks to which man thinks, feels and acts in the higher regions.

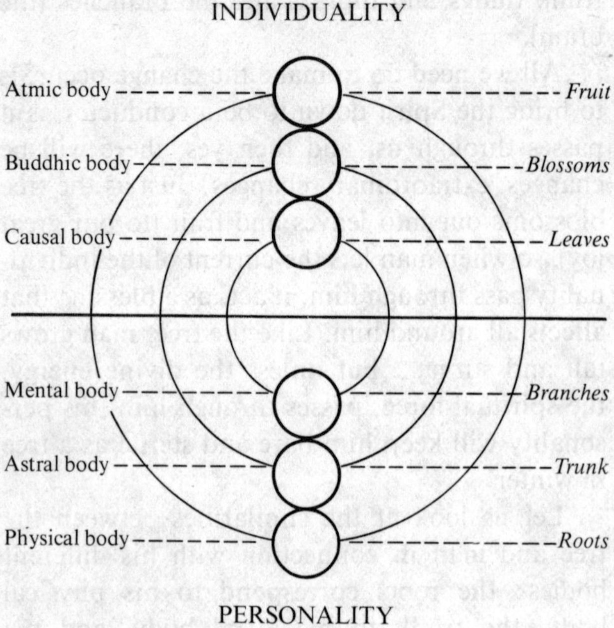

The personality and the individuality thus form two trinities. When the disciple finally allows the individuality to penetrate and dominate his personality, he joins the two trinities and becomes the Seal of Solomon, the complete being. That is our task : to bring the divine trinity down into us, to let the lower trinity become invaded and dominated by the higher trinity, so that it manifests through us and bears fruit, blossoms and leaves !

8

THE SILENT VOICE OF THE HIGHER SELF

At a time when it was more difficult to give humans an idea of psychology because they were not able to understand, the Initiates interpreted the higher and lower natures by the idea of angels and devils: a guardian angel stood at the right of man and a devil at his left, the angel to give him good counsel, the devil to lead him into error and make him a victim.

Now, is it true that we have a devil at our left and an angel at our right at all times? Well, I believe they are there, but in what form is another question. They are there in the form of our two natures, the only difference being that some people give the divine nature a chance to manifest itself and as a result receive guidance, enlightenment, illumination, revelations... and others do not. The ones who do are always in the clear, their thinking is lucid, their entire existence is enormously helped, they are comforted, sustained, protected. The other people prefer to abandon themselves to their instincts, their greed and lust, and all their actions result in disastrous consequences, whereupon they say they were tempted by the devil! In reality they were overcome by their own lower instincts, because they had no way of controlling them.

Even if there were neither Heaven nor Hell, nor Angels, nor demons, nor devils, one thing is certain: the two natures which constitute man are in constant opposition. No one, if he is honest, can refuse to admit that from time to time his higher Nature speaks to him and tries to stop him from doing something or going in one direction rather than another. Yes, the divine Nature whispers softly, delicately, without insistence, for it has the greatest respect for our freedom; never will it use violence, loud trumpets, or impose in any way on us: no, it murmurs its advice once or twice, so softly that a person who lacks the necessary discernment does not even realize the higher Nature is speaking to him.

The lower nature imposes itself, it gets its way night and day and is always arguing and recriminating. It knows how to send the brain a most learned and philosophical delegation to persuade it to go in the direction it wants, and most of the time it succeeds. How many people make the mistake of not being able to tell which of the two natures is speaking to them! They prefer noise to silence, and incline towards the personality without realizing how much of its advice is dangerous. They are blinded by its insistence, thinking it must be right if it insists so much! Unfortunately that is not the case.

The personality is clever and ingenious, it knows that if it makes a lot of noise it will bewilder people; it is afraid of silence because silence prevents it from being clever and arrogant, no one notices its demands and tempers, in the silence it is paralysed, choked, unable to find the right conditions for the execution of its plans. Silence is a door into the celestial regions, and the personality, whose plans are invariably egocentric, who is always pulling the cover over onto its own side, always ready to attack, to rebel and venge itself, knows that silence means the end of its reign, that it will have to capitulate... which it does not want to do! At the slightest irritation or contradiction, instead of remaining calm and silent, the personality says, "Hit him! Kill him!": the advice of the personality is what leads to war. The individuality advises us, "Wait a while, pray for your adversary, send him a few good thoughts and see if he doesn't change... in which case you will have made a friend instead of an enemy! There is nothing to worry about, no one has the power to destroy you, you are here for eternity! The thing is to try to have a little more light, a little more love!" That is the advice of the individuality. But the personality makes such a racket with its trumpets and big drums, it is so insistent all the time that man, who is in fact a little silly, a little stupid, says, "All right, all right, as you wish!" All the exercises practiced in an Initiatic School, such as meditation, concentration, prayer, have the same goal: to reduce the personality and to give the individuality, the spirit, more and more opportunities to express itself.

The personality loathes silence (what can silence do for you?) and so does a young person: he flares up very quickly, storms and tornadoes and hurricanes are constantly swirling around inside him, and the divine side is consequently unable to express itself. Years later, he permits a little silence to come into his life and consequently good qualities and virtues begin to manifest where before they could not. Like what happens in Nature – sometimes a plant starts to bloom before its time, that is, before the end of winter and, if the frost should come during the night, it will die. The plant's forces and energies cannot blossom if conditions are not favourable. Well, that is what happens to humans, as long as they are buffeted about by wild winds and storms, they cannot hear the inner voice of wisdom, the voice of the angels. First the passions must be appeased, and then the good qualities will have the right conditions to bloom.

I can give you an even better argument, stolen from geology, which also applies to the evolution of man. The earth at its origin was made of matter in a state of fusion, which made life as we know it impossible. Millions of years later the earth cooled off and its crust settled long enough to allow a few plants and animals to appear, but violent eruptions still shook the earth from time to time. Finally the crust became sufficiently thick and stable for the cataclysms to die out and the atmospheric conditions to become calmer; conditions became suitable for plants to appear and grab hold of the earth, followed by animals, and last of all, by man. When I see someone who is still in the state the earth was in long ago, I say to him, "My friend, the shining spirits above cannot come and install themselves in you because conditions are not right yet; they will come only when you become a little calmer, a little wiser."

You see, it is perfectly clear: once you create the inner silence, then in this silence, this calming of passions, the divine Self will be able to grow and blossom into virtue, beauty, light. Until then, you cannot expect anything: the invisible world is not stupid, the higher Beings would never install themselves where there is the risk of collapse at any moment!

Now let us take great artists for instance, or genuine clairvoyants, or mathematical geniuses: all have certain gifts. What is a gift? An entity which installs itself in you to help you and to work through you. Of course, psychologists will never accept this, but nevertheless talent and ability are entities that live in humans. The proof that it is not humans themselves who create miracles but higher Beings working through them, is the fact that these gifts can disappear. Often people lose a great gift,a great talent, as the result of leading a disorderly life.

Do you long to attract higher entities and have them bring you gifts and virtues? Introduce silence and harmony within! Only under those conditions will such entities manifest themselves. They are there, waiting, and when they see someone establish order and peace within himself, with what joy they rush to help him and others through him! Yes, that is something you do not know either. Why not work towards that goal, why live forever with the same chaos and racket, the same agitation?

If human beings knew more about the great Initiatic truths, they would be able to put so many things right inside themselves. Silence is the essential condition for the elimination of dissonance. In the silence, the harmonious silence, the Voice of God speaks to us, warns us, guides us, protects us. You cannot hear it? That is because of all the racket you make, not only in the physical plane but in your thoughts and feelings. When you calm down, when you accept to wait in silence, you will hear the Voice telling you that God is eternal, that He is the only One who can give you what you need: it is called the *Voice of Silence* and is the title of several books on the Eastern Wisdom. When a yogi reaches a state of calm, when he stops his thoughts (because, being movement, thoughts also make a noise), then he hears the Voice of Silence, the Voice of his divine Nature, his higher Self.

9

ONLY BY SERVING THE DIVINE NATURE

I

This question of the personality and the individuality is a problem that lasts a whole lifetime, and not only one life, but during all the rest of our incarnations. For the truth is that just when we think we are being truly inspired, we are most likely being misguided by the personality.

The individuality does its best to warn us of the consequences of our actions and the accidents that loom ahead, but instead of listening, we tell it to be quiet and not interfere. That is why the most important thing, our first task as a disciple, is to observe ourselves continually: each thought, each idea or desire that comes to us should make us pause and determine which nature is suggesting it, we must recognize what kind of impulse it is, and know which direction it will take us in. Very few ever make this effort, but let themselves be dragged down by the personality. Because they give in to the personality, they are constantly filled with disillusion and remorse. If you could see into people's hearts, if you received their confessions, you would be terrified as I often am at what I hear. The conclusion I come to is that people do not have a clear idea of the two natures constantly trying to express themselves in them.

Humans urge each other to satisfy their lower desires because they think they will be the ones to profit and enjoy the results, but it is not so! The only ones to profit are the ones they work for, which is something they do not realize until they have lost all their joy, their strength, their inspiration. The invisible entities in man come and feast themselves, unbeknownst to him. The day we realize this and understand that we have spent our lives working for others, not for our own benefit... that our divine Nature is not the one to be enriched, nor fulfilled, it will be too late. Who benefits, who are the "others"? It would take too long to explain now, but many entities feast themselves at our expense! Generations of humans have worked to satisfy them, and we are left with an inheritance that we drag along with us, myriad creatures who profit from the way we live, without our knowing it. Of course other creatures also exist in the invisible world. If we worked for them we would gain a great deal *ourselves*, because each effort to content and satisfy them would increase our patrimony, our wealth, our capital.

Those who observe themselves carefully see that after gratifying certain desires, they lose their peace of mind, their energy, their lucidity... which is proof that others were enjoying themselves in their stead; if we were clairvoyant at that time, we would see the millions and millions of creatures busy robbing us of our energies. You think everything you do under the impulse of the personality is done for your own welfare (which is why you are so insistent on obeying those impulses), but if you knew it was not for you, that millions of other beings both visible and invisible push you into doing these things, and that you work for them in their interest, not in yours, perhaps you would not be in such a hurry nor so convinced that you are right in everything you do. The whole point is to know when you are working for your benefit and when you are working for the lower entities or family spirits who ruin you. You must make every effort to dominate and control such entities, reducing them to silence, otherwise you are no more than an animal, a domesticated animal.

Yes, take animals: some live in liberty in the forest, but horses, cows, camels, dogs, usually work for a master, and the master generally exploits the poor things. We human beings are like those animals, in the employ of forces outside ourselves that we spend our lives working for.

Once I talked with a writer who had a high opinion of himself because he had written one or two novels. I was explaining this question of man's two natures, the lower and the higher Self, and when I said there were creatures in the invisible world who exploited us as we exploit animals, he was most indignant. "What!" he cried. "That is ridiculous." I looked at him thinking to myself that it was not terribly perspicacious on his part as a writer not to know that. It is certainly true that men make animals do their work for them and sell their skins without asking whether they have any right to do so. If the poor animals could express an opinion, they would no doubt complain of human injustice and cruelty, but we find it entirely natural. So do the beings who act the same way with us, to them it is logical to use us for their purposes. They hand us a bit of food and in exchange we work in their fields, till their land, obey them and carry out their projects, and in the end they cut us up to make ham and sausages and eat us for supper!

If we could peer into the invisible world and see the tribes and peoples who use human beings as we use... and devour... animals! One day, not only you, but all mankind will realize this.

It is very difficult to make humans understand that their physical body (the lower half) is not their true selves. One must, of course, feed it and keep it alive, as a rider feeds his mount, but we must not give it everything, nor above all, identify with it. If you think about this and meditate on the subject, you will be able to know in every one of life's circumstances which nature is urging you forward, the personality or the individuality. The time will come when you will have enough discernment, enough light, to realize that you have wasted all your time and energy, you have placed your capital in a bank that was not yours, and now it has all gone down the drain.

Take the question of sexuality. When you give in to love that is purely selfish and sensual, the action that follows takes place independently of you, regardless of your wishes, without your being able to stop it or refrain in any way. You can only stand by and observe, unable to control events, other forces take hold of you and run things. With spiritual love on the other hand, you know that you, your soul and spirit, your individuality or higher Self, the entire *you*, is nourished, and not other forces outside you, experiencing delight through you. It may be no more than a look, a word, a presence, a fragrance, a strain of music, but you are instantly elated, happy, ecstatic, knowing that your higher Self has been allowed to taste and breathe the most wonderful, delicate and nourishing of substances....

Unfortunately most people are not observant, they eat and drink and amuse themselves, convinced that if their physical body is satisfied they will be satisfied; they are not aware of the void in their soul and spirit. The physical body may be satisfied, sound asleep and snoring, but they remain starved, because the individuality received nothing at all!

You have to have acquired a certain degree of evolution to see the truth in what I am saying... you can talk all you like about spiritual love to a savage, sensual person, he will only say, "But if your sexual needs are not satisfied, you die! That is what makes us live!" Yes, it is certainly what brings life to the roots... but it kills the flowers above. Everything depends upon your degree of evolution.

II

Take a look at the human beings around you, observe their way of life, their work, their ideals, the goal they have chosen... what do you find? A lot of people doing all they can to gratify themselves, their desires and ambitions, without ever wondering whether those desires and ambitions are worth the trouble! Do you know anybody who asks God, "Am I in accord with *Thy* projects, O Lord? Am I doing *Thy* will or mine? What is *Thy* plan for us? Where and how should we work in order best to serve *Thee*?" Not many people bother to consider God's opinion.

The personality is what urges man to "live his own life", to lead that life according to his concepts and desires. That is the personality. The whole world tries its best to satisfy it without ever wondering if there might not be other projects a thousand times more important and sublime, projects that are divine, Cosmic projects. The nature of the individuality on the other hand, urges man to learn to decipher what Heaven's projects are and do his best to realize them. His life then changes completely: he ceases to cater to his weaknesses, illusions and appetites, and does his best to carry out God's plan. That is the beginning of the real life.

Of course it is difficult to know what God's plans are, but we could at least ask! Even if we cannot grasp them properly, we must beg Him to reveal them to us, "O Lord, if I cannot understand Thy plan, at least set me on the right path! Inspire me, even though blindly, even unknowingly to do Thy Will. Use me as Thou wilt, take over my will, live in me!"

Even if we do not know what God's Will is at a given moment, we know the general direction to go in... always toward what is good, what is difficult, what demands sacrifice, love and abnegation, generosity. But there are times when it is not possible to know exactly what God's Will is. Then, since we know that we lack clairvoyance and lucidity, we should ask Him, "Please God, in spite of me, push me, make me go where I can best serve Thee, so that Thy Will be done." Sometimes we realize God's projects blindly and afterwards we think about what we did and are surprised: "Goodness! What was this force that took over for me and used me? I saved all those people thinking I was doing wrong and now I see that the wrong was the best I have ever done!" It is not always given to those who serve God to be certain of their usefulness to Him.

Nevertheless, you should beg God to let you serve. Say, "I understand, I finally understand that it will never be possible to do anything with my lower nature. It is too headstrong, too stubborn and selfish, I cannot change it. Now, after all these wasted years, I finally understand, O God, that there is nothing I can do with the personality, I see that it is limited and narrow, blind and ill-intentioned. So, send me one of thy Heavenly Beings, a perfect creature to live in me and guide me, teach me and take over my life for me, so that I may realize Thy plans in spite of myself!"

That is the best of all prayers. The others all have something selfish to say, some personal slant, something to be gained, some personal purpose in mind... a desire to impress God, for instance, or buy Him... whereas all this one says is that you put your life into His hands. "I am ready to die, O Lord! Take my life, cause me to disappear if that will help... but send your celestial entities to replace my lower nature!" Then, because one gift deserves another, and because you have offered the most precious thing you have, Heaven is obliged to hear... you have paid ahead of time for what you are requesting! For even Heaven must be paid before you can receive, nothing is free, nothing. If you think you can obtain blessings from Heaven by doing senseless things all your life, you are wrong.

People pray for material advantages, which is why their prayers are not granted. But if you offer your soul, and ask for nothing in return but wisdom, love, peace, in exchange for your life, your total commitment... then the higher Beings will be moved to give you everything. As in a pawn shop: you give your watch, your ring or whatever, and in exchange you are given a few coins! On earth everything is a reflection: "That which is below is like that which is above".

Make up your mind, here and now, to ask God His opinion before making any decisions. Say, "Perhaps You have plans for me, perhaps I am standing in the way of these plans..." and then ask Him to forgive you, entreat Him to send the higher Beings to guide you. This light I am giving you will enable you to know exactly where you stand, whereas without the divine laws you are apt to spend your time thinking only of satisfying your lower nature, in which case make no mistake: the crowd may applaud you, you may have tremendous success in certain fields, but you will still be nothing much as far as the invisible world is concerned. Let the crowd be (a crowd is blind to the true values), do not let yourself be influenced by the crowd. Whether people carry you in triumph on their shoulders or throw tomatoes at you, you should remain indifferent, realizing their lack of criteria... you have the only absolute criteria.

If you work for Heaven, for the Truth, the Light, the Kingdom of God, then whatever happens to you, whatever people say or do to you, there is no reason to be afraid or discouraged: you are on the right road, you can be sure and certain of that. But if you retreat, if you give up, if you run no risk for the truth you seek and refuse to work for it, then you will be proving that your goal was a personal one, in your own interests only. Those who work for the truth, for the realization of God's great projects, are never afraid, never, no matter what happens to them. They can be persecuted, martyrized, put to death, still they go on believing they are immortal, and, that beyond this suffering, the reward of everlasting glory awaits them.

Humans tend to behave as though they could decide what is true or not: they accept that which stirs their applause or approval, and the rest, unless it is in conformance with what they imagine to be true, they reject as being false or stupid. How many times do I see this! People refusing to budge from their convictions, their needs and appetites, struggling to the end to protect and preserve them as though their salvation depended on it! Everyone does that to a certain extent, you think, everyone is ready to fight for old outworn concepts! Well, I judge the grandeur of a person by how willing he is to sweep aside his ideas in exchange for a divine philosophy. You too, instead of holding on to your ideas and opinions and rejecting whatever does not suit you, you too must decide to change and do the reverse. If you want to evolve, now is the time to give up your mistaken ideas and conform once and for all, to the Divine Philosophy.

10

ADDRESS THE HIGHER SELF IN OTHERS

I

Since the world is always imagining, since everyone in it dreams, desires, imagines all kinds of things, we think we know what imagination is. But real imagination, imagination according to the Initiate's understanding of the word, is the creative faculty which allows us to realize our finest aspirations.

Imagination can be compared to a woman. After receiving the seed from her husband, instantly she goes to work shaping and building her future child, whose character and form will correspond exactly with the seed's contents. Imagination is a woman, she produces, she materializes what she receives! Thus, if you concentrate on the higher world and higher Beings, your imagination will capture the realities of that world and those Beings and bring them to life for you, *realize* them for you. Every human being has a wife, his imagination, but, because he has no idea how to work with her nor what she can be asked to do, he brings monsters into the world. If humans were conscious and vigilant, if they knew what to do, their imagination would produce nothing but geniuses! "As ye sow, so shall ye reap."

The power of the imagination is tremendous. If you do not obtain results it is because you are not consistent. Or,you may long to develop and manifest your virtues, but as you have not learned to dominate your lower impulses, they go on occupying your imagination, destroying your good work. To obtain results from your highest, most divine desires, you must work consciously, intelligently and methodically. The truth is that no desire, good or bad, remains unrealized. From the moment you feel it, instantly it is realized in the subtle world, but for it to be realized on the physical plane it must become visible and tangible, and that takes time, sometimes years, even centuries. If you are patient and if you remain concentrated on one splendid idea until your imagination actually condenses it and brings it to life, it will be both visible and tangible. Imagination attracts the elements that correspond to her desires, she uses them to explore the depths of the ocean and the heights of the heavens; she accumulates ideas and desires and one day they become concrete, realized in matter.

Is it not wonderful to know that everything you hope for will one day be yours? If you imagine you are perfect, that you have every virtue, it will help you to attain perfection; as long as man goes on thinking he is as he appears to be at the moment, he will be held back on the lower stages of evolution, for this mediocre, insignificant image of himself has an effect on him, it keeps him from advancing. Whereas if he has a glorious mental image of himself on which to concentrate, this image will affect him by provoking other vibrations and other impulses. Because he wants to attain that image, he advances. Otherwise he stagnates and never becomes aware of his true identity, true reality.

You say, "What reality? I am reality!" No, that reality is illusory. The true reality is divine, that is reality. What we think of as reality is an illusion, a lie. Thus we cannot know reality until we idealize and divinize all creatures including ourselves. That is what the Indians call Jnani-Yoga. Jnani-Yoga is no more than the process of idealization. The disciple seeks to know himself because he wants to reach God Himself, to be able to say as Jesus said, "My Father and I are one", "I am He". A disciple seeks his divine Nature, his real Self. By creating an image of himself which includes everything perfect and by feeding this image and strengthening it daily, little by little it becomes part of him and compels him to improve.

Once a being has succeeded in creating a divine image of himself, this image will have a beneficial influence on all living creatures, on animals, plants and stones, on all Nature, because he will be emitting rays of light, forces and vibrations that bring order, balance, and harmony wherever he goes.

How many people wish more than anything to be loved and do everything in their power to make it happen, but unfortunately they do everything externally, without realizing that to be loved they must change their vibrations and become more gentle, more peaceful, more harmonious. And this is only possible when you have a divine image of yourself.

Of course if you forget that this is an exercise and think of yourself as having already attained your image of perfection, you will only make yourself ridiculous and unbearable to others. You must work on your divine image in the invisible world and not imagine you are divine here on earth... otherwise the others will say, "There goes an idiot who thinks he's perfect", and they will be right!

However gigantic a task you undertake inwardly, go on behaving as simply as possible with others, being careful not to provoke any negative reactions. Imagine you are beautiful, radiant with light, just as you were in the remote past when you were with God all the time, and just as you will be in the future when you are perfect, but never forget that it is not yet so on the physical plane.

All the splendour, all the treasures we possess above must be brought down and materialized on the physical plane. Heaven is the world of ideas in which everything is beautiful and perfect, and we must bring it down on earth, that is, into our physical bodies, to replace every particle with indestructible, crystal-clear, immortal particles. That is the sublime, glorious task. No one, or nearly no one, bothers to imagine this work, much less undertake it, and yet it is the *only* work we are called upon to do.

II

Most people have the habit of seeing only the bad side in other people and things, and the one who finds the most faults in others is considered the most intelligent. Well, I think that on the contrary, the most intelligent man is the one who tries his best to find the good that exists in all people. It is true that one runs the risk with this attitude of falling into traps and having to pay very dearly. Human nature is wicked at heart, religion tells us that, so why deceive ourselves? Well, my answer is that you should go further in your studies : man has a lower nature, it is true, it manifests itself all too often... but he also has a higher Nature which one sees rarely, but which exists and will appear and express itself if given the proper conditions.

It is not by deciding once and for all that human nature is evil that one prepares the best conditions for the manifestation of the higher Self! You must not think an Initiate, a seer, does not see the bad side in those around him, he sees it, his eyes are trained to see it, but he does not stop there as others do, he knows that he cannot help someone by dwelling on their faults and vices... that attitude only makes them worse.

An Initiate knows that men and women are God's children, His sons and daughters, and that is what he concentrates on, that is the idea he has in mind when he meets people. It is a creative work he does, for he transforms people and is himself happy as a result! Believe me, that is the best way to be with others: seek to discover their qualities and virtues, their assets, and concentrate on them. Sometimes those aspects are so well camouflaged that even the person involved is not aware of them... you must form the habit of looking into the depths *behind* people's superficial, visible manifestations, which can be enormously deceptive.

It is so easy to find fault! But to discern virtues that are not yet manifested, you must know an entire science. Each one of you has divine qualities which are waiting for the time when they can appear, and that is what I am busy doing, that is what I am interested in, I look for the hidden qualities that have not yet appeared. In that way I work on you and on myself at the same time, and you should do the same. You should entertain only the most sacred thoughts for each other and gradually stop thinking about the details which are far from glorious, dwelling only on the sacred, divine Principle that exists in all creatures. Yes, why not have the most sacred feelings for everything divine, immortal, eternal in man? In that way you will be working divinely on yourself as well as really helping others. Whereas when you think only about their faults, you do yourself harm because, besides feeding on filth, you keep others from evolving. How ignorant! You think you can make others correct themselves by underlining their faults and failings, but actually it is the opposite that happens. Humans are wicked, cruel and anything else you wish, it is true, but that is no reason to spend your life seeing only that side and talking about that and nothing else. You should open your eyes, of course, but that is only half your task. If someone is busy stealing from you or plotting to ruin you, it is better to take notice, but there is no point in stopping there, you must see further, "Poor thing," you could say, "He is that way now because he has not had much time to improve himself, but if I concentrate on his spirit, on the Divine in him, he will begin to change!" That is, in any case, the work a Master does on his disciples and in that way he accelerates their evolution.

Evidently if your reason for not liking someone is that he has wronged you or been dishonest with you, it will be difficult for you to see the divine spark in him! But if you love him already, you have no need to force yourself, he is divine as far as you are concerned. The difficulty exists only when you do not love him, and that is where you must adopt a method of work which you will use consciously, knowing how beneficial the results will be for both of you. In order to do that, however, you cannot live exclusively on the emotional, sentimental level, you must know how to reason and control your emotions, knowing that if you are forever concentrating on someone's faults, you will always be on the same level, the same diapason with that person, you will even attract his faults to yourself... and be even more unjust, dishonest or vicious than he. You criticize him, and yet you are worse than he is!

I know that everything I say will not be accepted today, but in the future you will learn to work this way, mentally projecting your parents, your friends and everyone you meet (even your enemies) into the higher regions. Yes, in the future, we will all think only about the higher Nature, the Divine Nature in all people.

When you talk about someone's qualities, try to exaggerate a little and err on the good side... this will not really be exaggerating, because you are speaking of his Divine side. Usually when you talk about someone you are not actually talking about *him*, but about his sex, his stomach or intestines, his feet, etc. Nevertheless we are divinities, it says so in the Psalms: "Ye are gods"... why do we not manifest ourselves as gods? That side of us is buried somewhere, deeply buried under layers of impurity. We cannot see it, but it is there and must now be allowed to appear.

11

MAN'S RETURN TO GOD, THE VICTORY

People say, "If I am not the one to do it first, he'll do it to me", or "If I don't destroy him, he'll destroy me". This may be true wherever the law of the jungle reigns, but is that any reason for humans to devour each other in hatred, simply because creatures in swamps and jungles do it? We find it perfectly normal to tear each other apart because we have been taught certain expressions such as "Dog eat dog!", "Man's inhumanity to man", etc... and it is true that in the world, egoism, hatred and cruelty prevail. But the higher you climb the more you see manifestations of love, sacrifice and abnegation. The world is a theatre of war and strife, but if you climb up to the sun, the symbol of God in Heaven, you will behold love, light, peace. Those who claim the universe is governed by the law of the jungle may think they are right but, as their vision is confined to the lower regions, they are only fifty percent right!

Our heads are full of formulas which are not true for the most part and, by spreading half-truths, people destroy things that are true and good; influenced into seeing one side only, they do not see the other sublime nature that is not developed, simply because man does not cultivate it. Being almost completely subject to the personality, he is used to thinking, "If I don't eat them they will eat me." That is the law of the jungle: take, devour, kill!

Now, if man were willing to do a little work, to make a few efforts to put his other, divine Nature, now lying dormant, in first place, what would happen? The higher Nature, the individuality, would absorb all the evil in him. If you think the individuality goes without food, you are in error: it eats, and turns what it eats into light!

Now, here is an explanation on the subject of food. When a criminal eats food, because the food has divine properties, he receives strength from it... reinforcing his wickedness and destructiveness. Why does the food not improve him rather than increase his wickedness? Because when we eat, we transform the elements in the food into our own nature. It all depends, our lives depend, on the state we are in when we eat, for, as we assimilate it, the food becomes what we are. People who are wicked do not become good by eating, they become stronger in their desire to do evil, and good people become stronger in their desire to do good. Food is transformed into each creature's own nature as he consumes it. Initiates pray, "Lord, take my life, I give it to Thee to be absorbed and used: let there be nothing left of me but Thee!" They pray God, not to be annihilated, but to be transformed into His substance, to be one with God's Nature.

All truly spiritual people understand that their supreme desire is to be consumed by God; they offer themselves in sacrifice. We do not understand the word "sacrifice", it terrifies us because it is connected in our minds with pain and death. In the lower regions this is true, if man is devoured by the lower entities, he is lost. But once you give yourself to the celestial Beings, you become richer, more beautiful, more youthful and strong: you are resuscitated! There is no need to fear, if you have the courage to offer yourself and your life to Heaven, your personality will be utterly consumed, there will be not a trace left, and you will be able to say with the Initiates, "Not I (the personality), but Christ in me (the individuality) leads me and lights my way."

This idea of the personality and the individuality is nothing but another way of giving you the truth, I am giving you the very same truths you find in the Bible, only my way of expressing these truths is slightly different. To be "eaten" by glorious entities is the greatest joy, indescribably blissful! All religions teach man to offer himself to God in sacrifice, it is the image which best demonstrates the spiritual ideal of becoming one with God and living in His Bosom throughout Eternity.

The ancients sacrificed animals... sometimes even humans (hecatombs are frequently mentioned in the Old Testament), and the Bible says that the smoke from these sacrifices was pleasing to God's nostrils. What was meant by the sacrifices and why, with the coming of Jesus, did this custom cease? Because man was no longer asked to sacrifice his cattle but rather his inner animals, his vices, passions and lust, his sensuality. That is the real sacrifice, to transform brute instinct into pure, light-filled energy.

Each year at the Ceremony of the Fire, at Michaelmas, I explain the meaning of the sacrifice taking place before you: the logs, the twisted ugly branches of dead wood in the fire become transformed by the flames into light and heat. If we do not understand this principle and refuse to offer ourselves in sacrifice to be "eaten" by our Lord, we remain as dead wood. Those who beg to be consumed by the fire, the sublime fire of divine love, not only never die, they are resuscitated. That is the meaning of "Unless ye die ye shall not live." We must die, but how? Not with a knife or gun of course. Jesus was not talking about physical death but of dying unto the personality, the lower world of desire and vices, so that we might come to life on the higher plane, that of the individuality. That is when the individuality is nourished.

Usually it is the personality that is nourished, because it feeds on us... that is its pleasure, to seize and devour us. Twenty, thirty, fifty times a day we are cornered and eaten by the personality! When we become too weak to object (whilst it becomes enormously strengthened), it tells us what to do. Even then, if we know how to summon the individuality to our aid, as it too is hungry, as it too knows how to nourish itself, in no time nothing will be left of the personality!

Now let me ask you to be very clear in your minds about one thing: you will never succeed in transforming your lower nature, the personality. No matter how hard you try, no matter what superhuman efforts you make, you will never change it. The only thing to do, the only way to change, is to give your divine Nature, the individuality or higher Self, the chance to absorb the personality, to make it disappear.

The lower nature, as I have told you, is an

emanation of the higher Nature. Because man was curious and wanted to have a greater knowledge of life and the universe, he left Paradise where he lived with God, and descended into matter. This descent is called *involution.* It was accomplished at the expense of man's radiation, his lightness, for he was compelled to take on the density and weight of the lower bodies, the mental, astral and physical bodies. But it is also a fact that man is predestined to return to his original country, his celestial abode, and that ascent is called *evolution.* When he abandons his lower bodies and lives only in his higher bodies, the Causal, Buddhic and Atmic bodies, he becomes a divinity. The earth (whose evolution takes place simultaneously and along parallel lines with man's evolution) will then lose its density and heaviness, it will become transparent, radiant with light, and all will melt into the Heart of God and be one with Him.

That is the Teaching of the Initiates, the Initiatic Science. It will not happen for a few million years, do not worry! If it makes you anxious, realize that so much time has to elapse before the world can change that you will be sick and tired of the world as it is, and you will want it to happen. What I am saying agrees with all the esoteric, religious traditions, they all teach that man must become once again what he was originally. For the moment he is caught somewhere between Heaven and Hell, having erred for so long and changed his abode so often he no longer knows where to go. He has forgotten all the ancient knowledge, and that is why he needs a guide; in the past he was guided by his own light, but now he has lost it, he cannot see. Of course people do exist who remember the way it was originally, they know where they come from and where they are going, their inner light guides them. With each passing day they are confirmed in the truth of the ancient knowledge they once knew, their certainty grows and grows... they know the light will never lead them astray.

But, except for this minority of seers, sages and wise men, most humans live out their lives torn between uncertainty and anguish, wondering what is the meaning of life and what happens after death, and this uncertainty is reflected in everything, the way they live, their literature and their art, which actually demolish the little bit of hope and faith they might have left! And those are the works the younger generation prefers to the works of people who have found the light and recorded their experiences. Writers, philosophers, scholars alike are guilty of putting out the light man once had, and now, because of their ignorance, mankind has lost its way, it has no idea what direction to go in... it needs to be shown the path. Those who understand will make the decision at once, the others will have to go through many experiences, but sooner or later all will understand.

Now, here is what I want to tell you: you should get down on your knees and thank God that you are in this Initiatic School, where you are given the answers to all your problems as well as the methods to help you solve them. In this way you cannot fail, you will become gradually happier and happier, richer and richer in virtue and qualities!

By the same author:

Izvor Collection

201 – TOWARD A SOLAR CIVILISATION

Although we may know about heliocentricity from the point of view of astronomy, we are still far from having exhausted all its possibilities in the biological, psychological, cultural and spiritual spheres. We are constantly looking for more effective ways of harnessing solar energy: why not look for traces of the sun buried deep in man's psychic structure and consequently in human society? The sun exists within each one of us and if allowed to, can manifest its presence by awakening our consciousness to a global view of human problems.

202 – MAN, MASTER OF HIS DESTINY

Why is one born in a particular country and a particular family? Why is one healthy, rich, illustrious and powerful, or on the contrary poor, handicapped and miserable? The bonds one forges with others almost without realizing it, where do they spring from and why? Even those who think they are entirely free must put up with their fate because of their ignorance of the laws which govern the invisible world. By revealing these laws, the Master not only helps the disciple to unravel the tangled threads of his life, he also gives him the tools he must have in order to become master of his own destiny.

203 – EDUCATION BEGINS BEFORE BIRTH

Is it possible for education to begin before birth? Yes. Because true education is primarily subconscious. A child is not a little animal which you can start training as soon as it is old enough. A child in the womb is a soul and its mother can have a beneficial influence on it even at this stage, through the harmony of her thoughts, acts and feelings. And this pre-natal influence which, in essence, is a form of magic, must be faithfully continued once the baby is born, for, as all parents should realize, a tiny baby is highly sensitive to both its physical and spiritual environment. It is by their own example that parents and teachers can best succeed in their task of educating the child. He is far more deeply impressed by the way the people around him behave and are, than by any lesson or advice that he receives from time to time. Educating the child's subconscious requires a very high level of consciousness on the part of the educators.

204 – THE YOGA OF NUTRITION

This book is not a dietary handbook, it has nothing to do with diet. The Master Omraam Mikhaël Aïvanhov considers the way man thinks about the food more important than what, or how much, he eats. The Master lifts the act of eating onto the level of a mystical rite, a sacrament such as Holy Communion, the Last Supper, in all their spiritual significance.

Even someone to whom the spiritual aspect is foreign cannot but understand as he reads that his thoughts and feelings, his way of considering his daily nourishment, are what lead him to the profound mysteries of the relationship between man and Nature, the nature which nourishes him. If he deepens that relationship by extracting from the food the more subtle, finer elements, his entire being will then be able to unfold and flourish.

205 – SEXUAL FORCE OR THE WINGED DRAGON

The dragon, fabulous beast of Mythology and all Christian iconography, is not merely a relic of antiquity but a symbol of the human being's instinctive, primitive forces. The spiritual life is the process of learning how to subdue, control and direct these forces so that man will be propelled to the highest peaks of spirituality. The fire-breathing monster with the tail of a serpent has wings as well, indicating that the forces he embodies have a spiritual destination. The Master Omraam Mikhaël Aïvanhov says, "Sexual energy can be compared to petrol: if you are ignorant and careless you are burned by it, your very quintessence will be destroyed by this consuming force. The Initiates are those whose knowledge permits them to use the force to soar above the universe." That is the true meaning of the winged Dragon.

206 – THE UNIVERSAL WHITE BROTHERHOOD IS NOT A SECT

The very strong feelings of antipathy held by many of the general public on the subject of sects tend to hide the real problems of society. Indignation is felt against minorities who have decided to undertake a spiritual life apart from orthodox religious practice but non-conformity in other fields is looked upon with favour. The intellectual, political, social and economic fields are largely composed of many separate parts and groups which are, in effect, 'sects,' concerned with the triumph of their own particular theories or interests over those of their opponents. From now on a sect will no longer be defined in relation to the official church but in terms of the universality of its ideas in all fields. And if the Universal White Brotherhood is not a sect, it is precisely because its Teaching, which is directed to men of every race and religion and which encompasses every kind of human activity, aims at developing a consciousness of universality amongst all men.

207 – WHAT IS A SPIRITUAL MASTER?

Although the idea of a spiritual Master is becoming more and more familiar to the public, the nature and role of a Master are still poorly understood, even by those who claim to be disciples. The purpose of this book is essentially to shed light on the subject. This clarification may seem ruthless to some, but it is necessary, for what matters above all is not to delude oneself as to the realities of the spiritual life. It is true that a Master is that prodigious being capable of leading men towards the highest summits of the spirit, but for the Master as for his disciples, this exciting adventure can be successful only if it is accompanied by tremendous demands upon oneself.

208 – UNDER THE DOVE, THE REIGN OF PEACE

All the official steps taken in favour of peace seem to infer that it is a state which can be imposed on men from the outside... the creating of organizations for peace, reinforcing security means, the imprisonment or pure and simple suppression of troublemakers, for example. But what hope is there for peace when man continues to nourish within himself the seeds of all political, social and economic conflicts? These seeds are his uncontrolled desires for possession and domination. A better understanding of what peace truly is and the conditions necessary for achieving it are called for. As long as man doesn't make the decision to intervene on the battlefield of his disorderly thoughts and feelings, he won't be able to create a lasting peace.

209 – CHRISTMAS AND EASTER IN THE INITIATIC TRADITION

The Feasts of Christmas and Easter, celebrated annually throughout Christendom to commemorate the birth and resurrection of Jesus, actually are part of the initiatic tradition in existence long before the Christian era. Their appearance at those particular times of the year – the Winter solstice and the Spring equinox – is indicative of their Cosmic significance and also of the fact that man participates in the processes of gestation, birth and blossoming which take place in nature.

Christmas and Easter, the second birth and the resurrection, are really two different ways of celebrating the regeneration of man and his birth into the spiritual world.

210 – THE TREE OF THE KNOWLEDGE OF GOOD AND EVIL

The existence of evil in a world created by God who is perfect is an enigma which remains unsolved to this day by the world's philosophies or religions. Within the framework of Judeo-Christianism, Master Omraam Mikhaël Aïvanhov asserts that the solution lies in knowing what methods to use to contain evil, rather than in explanations or interpretations. Whatever its origin, evil is a reality which man confronts daily, both inwardly and outwardly. He must learn to deal with it. For him to fight against it is useless, even dangerous, for the odds are against him. He must be armed with *methods* of dealing with it, to overcome and transform it. This book offers those methods.

211 – FREEDOM, THE SPIRIT TRIUMPHANT

Freedom has become such a political stake that we have lost sight of the true terms through which man can find freedom. It is those terms, which are those of the relationship between spirit and matter, that the Master Omraam Mikhaël Aïvanhov attempts to restore. "No creature," he says, "can subsist without a certain number of elements that he receives from outside himself. God alone is not subject to this law; He has no need of anything external to Himself. But He has left a spark of Himself, a spirit identical to Him in nature, in every human being, and therefore man, thanks to his spirit, can create everything he needs. The Teaching I bring is that of the spirit, the Creator, and not that of matter and of creation. This is why I tell you that by entering the realm of the spirit which creates, forms and shapes matter, we will escape the hold the outside world has on us and be free." *(forthcoming)*

212 – LIGHT IS A LIVING SPIRIT

Light offers infinite possibilities to us in the material and spiritual fields. It is seen by tradition as the living substance with which God created the world and in the last few years we have seen the development of the laser with all its potential. Omraam Mikhaël Aïvanhov invites us in this book to discover light's spiritual possibilities, to see how it can protect, nourish and teach us to know ourselves, nature and God, but above all he shows light as the only truly effective method of transforming ourselves and the world.

213 – MAN'S TWO NATURES, HUMAN AND DIVINE

To justify their failings and weaknesses, you hear people exclaim, "I'm only human!" What they should actually be saying is, "I'm only animal!" How, then, should we define human nature?

Man, that ambiguous creature placed by evolution on the border between the animal world and the divine world, has a double nature. To be able to advance further in his evolution he must become aware of this ambivalence. It says in the Holy Writ, "Ye are gods," which ought to remind man of the presence within of the higher essence which he must learn to manifest. "That is the real meaning of destiny," says Master Omraam Mikhaël Aïvanhov, "the true purpose and goal of our existence." This is why he comes back again and again to this question, giving us methods for us to learn and use in order to manifest ourselves as the gods we really are... but do not know yet.

(forthcoming)

[illegible] certain number of elements, that bodies [illegible] made [illegible]. If God [illegible] [illegible], He [illegible] need of [illegible] extended Himself [illegible] Himself [illegible] so as [illegible] being, and [illegible] spirit [illegible] create [illegible] of the spirit [illegible] matter and [illegible] between the [illegible] and [illegible] matter [illegible] world [illegible]

[illegible] DYNAMISM

Light [illegible] to [illegible] and spiritual fields. [illegible] with [illegible] the world [illegible] years [illegible] development of [illegible] potential [illegible] to discover [illegible] can [illegible] and God [illegible] as the only and effective method of transforming [illegible] and the world.

[illegible] NATURES [illegible] HUMAN [illegible]

[illegible] natures and [illegible] human [illegible] should [illegible] [illegible] should we [illegible] human [illegible]

Man [illegible] creature of [illegible] between [illegible] and [illegible] might [illegible] able [illegible] advance further in the [illegible] become aware of this [illegible] in [illegible] Holy [illegible] with [illegible] present [illegible] of [illegible] to [illegible] [illegible] [illegible] of the [illegible] back again [illegible] [illegible] selves [illegible] really are [illegible]

Distributed by:

AUSTRIA	PRADEEP – Siebenbrunnenfeldgasse 4 A - 1050 Wien
BELGIUM	VANDER S.A. – Av. des Volontaires 321 B - 1150 Bruxelles
BRITISH ISLES	PROSVETA Ltd. – 4 St. Helena Terrace Richmond, Surrey TW9 1NR Trade orders to: ELEMENT Books Ltd – The Old Brewery Tisbury, Salisbury, Wiltshire SP3 6NH
CANADA	PROSVETA Inc. – 1565 Montée Masson Duvernay est, Laval, Que. H7E 4P2
FRANCE	Editions PROSVETA S.A. – B.P. 12 83601 Fréjus Cedex
GERMANY	URANIA – Rudolf Diesel Ring 26 D - 8029 Sauerlach
GREECE	PROSVETA HELLAS 90 Bd. Vassileos Constantinou Le Pirée
IRELAND	PROSVETA IRELAND 24 Bompton Green Castleknock, Dublin
ITALY	PROSVETA – Bastelli 7 I - 43036 Fidenza (Parma)
PORTUGAL	Edições IDADE D'OURO Rua Passos Manuel 20 – 3.° Esq. P - 1100 Lisboa
SPAIN	PROSVETA ESPAÑOLA – Caspe 41 Barcelona – 10
SWITZERLAND	PROSVETA Société Coopérative CH - 1801 Les Monts-de-Corsier
UNITED-STATES	PROSVETA U.S.A. – 3964 Ince Blvd. Culver City, California 90230

Enquiries should be addressed to the nearest distributor

PRINTED IN FRANCE
APRIL 1984
PROSVETA EDITIONS, FRÉJUS

– N° d'impression : 1330 –
Dépôt légal : Avril 1984
Printed in France